Scott Foresman

Kindergarten Unit and End-of-Year Benchmark Assessments
Teacher's Manual

Reading STREET

Grade **K**

PEARSON

Glenview, Illinois • Boston, Massachusetts • Chandler, Arizona • Upper Saddle River, New Jersey

The Pearson Promise

As the largest educational publishing company in the world, Pearson is committed to providing you with curriculum that not only meets the Common Core State Standards, but also supports your implementation of these standards with your students.

Pearson has aligned the Common Core State Standards to every grade level of *Scott Foresman Reading Street,* our premier educational curriculum. This product provides an alignment of the Common Core State Standards to the kindergarten assessment items in *Scott Foresman Reading Street Unit and End-of-Year Benchmark Tests.*

We value your partnership highly and look forward to continuing our mission to provide educational materials that fully satisfy your classroom needs.

ISBN-13: 978-0-328-68390-1
ISBN-10:   0-328-68390-6
8 9 10 V001 15 14 13

Contents

OVERVIEW

Scott Foresman *Reading Street* provides a wide array of group-administered formal tests and classroom assessments to support instruction. This Teacher's Manual provides information and directions for administering and scoring the Kindergarten Unit and End-of-Year Benchmark Assessments aligned to Common Core State Standards, as well as other forms that may be copied and used with children in the classroom. Consumable Kindergarten Benchmark Assessment booklets are also available.

There are six Kindergarten Unit Benchmark Assessments, one for each of the six units. The content of these tests is based on targeted skills taught in each unit in these different areas:

Comprehension	Writing
Phonemic Awareness	Word Knowledge
Phonics	Word Reading

The End-of-Year Benchmark Test Assessment follows the same design as the Unit Benchmark Assessments, but it has more items. It measures selected skills from all six units taught during the year.

The primary purpose of the Kindergarten Unit and End-of-Year Benchmark Assessments is to help you collect information about individual children's reading, writing, and language skills development at the end of each unit and at the end of the school year. This information can be used to make instructional decisions about each child, identify specific strengths and weaknesses, and assess children's progress throughout the year.

USING THESE ASSESSMENTS

The Kindergarten Unit Benchmark Assessments are designed to be administered at the end of each unit. The End-of-Year Benchmark Assessment is a useful summative tool. Assessment tasks can be given to individuals, small groups, or the whole class—depending on the nature of each activity.

Since children will be more capable or less capable of handling these assessments at different times, teachers should use their own professional judgment in determining when to conduct assessments and how many parts of the assessments to administer.

Later sections of this Teacher's Manual provide guidelines and directions for administering and scoring each Benchmark Assessment. Each task in the Benchmark Assessment is designed to be administered in one sitting. You may administer more than one task in a sitting. If a child cannot manage a given task, you may move on to a different task or discontinue the assessment at that point.

SCORING THE ASSESSMENTS

For each task in the Unit and End-of-Year Benchmark Assessments, the directions include guidelines for scoring and evaluating each child's performance. Each assessment is designed to be scored by skill, and the results are based on a 3-point rating scale. Points on the scale can generally be defined as follows:

Proficient (+)   The child answers all questions correctly; additional practice should be challenging.

Developing (✓)   The child answers most questions correctly; additional practice should be guided.

Emerging (–)   The child answers few questions correctly, showing signs of beginning to understand the skill; additional practice should be targeted.

In a Phonics activity, for example, a child who answers five out of five questions correctly would receive a "Proficient" rating. A child who answers three or four of the five questions correctly would receive a "Developing" rating. Children who answer fewer than three questions correctly would be rated "Emerging." Specific criteria for all three ratings are provided with each assessment task.

At the end of the directions for each Unit and the End-of-Year Benchmark Assessment, you will find an evaluation chart that may be copied for classroom use. The **Individual Record** may be used to record the results of the Benchmark Assessments for each child. At the back of this Teacher's Manual, you will find a Class Record chart. The **Class Record** (T97) may be used to record results on any assessment for all children in the class. Both of these charts will assist you in determining instructional needs for the children in your class.

INTERPRETING THE RESULTS

Each Unit Benchmark Assessment measures different skills. Since every assessed skill may be considered essential to the child's progress in later units, a child's performance should be evaluated on the basis of each skill. However, the following guidelines may help to interpret a child's performance on all the skills assessed in each unit:

- A child who receives a "Proficient" rating on all or most of the tasks in a unit is likely to need additional challenges in the course of instruction.

- A child who receives a "Developing" rating on most of the tasks in a unit will most likely benefit from guided instruction in the next unit.

- A child who receives an "Emerging" rating on three or more skills in a unit may need targeted instruction in specific concepts and skills.

Specific criteria for interpreting results in each task are provided in later sections of this Teacher's Manual.

ASSISTING ENGLISH LANGUAGE LEARNERS

While the Benchmark Assessments provide teachers with a way to measure children's progress on a unit-by-unit basis, the Benchmark Assessments also provide an opportunity for teachers to help English language learners become familiar with the linguistic patterns and structures they will encounter while taking state tests. The format of the Benchmark Assessments is similar to the format of the state tests, with similar directions, question stems, answer formats, and markings to "stop."

Among assessment tools, standardized tests cause teachers of English language learners the most concern. State tests, considered "high stakes," may be used to evaluate the effectiveness of the curriculum, the teacher, or the instructional approach. They are used to evaluate children's overall progress. High-stakes tests are typically designed and normed for proficient speakers of English. By providing opportunities for children to become familiar with the formats and language of the Benchmark Assessments, teachers assist English language learners in obtaining results that reflect children's learning of targeted skills rather than their aptitude for comprehending test language and formats. Teachers can use specific strategies to prepare English language learners for assessment. Using these strategies on the Benchmark Assessments will increase children's comfort levels and success with assessment tools such as the state tests.

Testing Strategies for All English Language Learners
Provide Accommodations for Children's Success

Any accommodations appropriate for English language learners should address children's linguistic needs, either directly or indirectly. As you consider accommodations for children taking the Benchmark Assessments, remember that when the state tests are given, no special accommodations are allowed. Therefore, as you make accommodations for English language learners, keep in mind that the ultimate goal is for these children to handle mainstream testing settings, terminology, and instruction, so any accommodations that you provide should be considered stepping stones to children's eventual successful encounter with mainstream testing conditions.

1. **Simplify and clarify directions.** Providing directions in simplified formats can reduce the language load for English language learners and help them focus solely on the task and targeted skill for the specific question(s). A good rule of thumb is to match the language used with the test to the language used with instruction. It is helpful to children when you replace complex English words with simpler English words that they are already familiar with or can grasp more easily. It is never appropriate, however, to translate test directions into children's first languages. This practice will not benefit children when they encounter state tests. (*See page T8,* **A Word of Caution**). However, you may ask children to restate directions in their own words so that you are sure they understand them.

2. **Provide a setting consistent with the instructional setting.** Administering tests in an alternate, smaller, even one-on-one, setting can allow for verbal scaffolding and provide English language learners with a setting that is comfortable and familiar to them. Be sure that the alternate setting is a setting with which children are familiar. Move children to mainstream testing settings when you feel they are ready.

3. **Consider timing.** Provide additional testing time and allow frequent or extended breaks during testing. On the Benchmark Assessments, each task is designed to be administered in one sitting of five to ten minutes. Children may benefit from your administering each task on a different day or after a significant break. If a child cannot manage a given task, you may move on to a different task or discontinue the assessment at that point. Keep in mind, however, that while this type of accommodation is used for all children in mainstream classrooms, it is important to be sure that English language learners are receiving the necessary linguistic support in English.

4. **Read aloud repeatedly.** When listening comprehension is assessed, it is valid to reread the selections aloud several times to aid children's understanding before proceeding to the questions, especially in the early units. Remember, however, that you are always moving toward the goal of having children listen to the comprehension selection only once.

A Word of Caution: In providing accommodations to children, it is important not to compromise the intent of the assessments. For example, it is never appropriate to translate into children's home languages the tested vocabulary in Rhyming or High-Frequency Words assessments. This practice alters the constructs of the assessments which are designed to measure both phonological awareness and word recognition. Similarly, it is never appropriate to translate listening comprehension selections into children's home languages. These assessments test both word recognition and understanding, so translating selections for children actually changes the intent of these tests.

Following the administration of the assessments, it is important to note which accommodations were used for English language learners and to interpret scores with that information in mind. As children progress in their English language skills and become more comfortable with assessment, it is important to reconsider accommodations that were given on previous assessments.

Familiarize Children with Academic Language and Test Language

The Benchmark Assessments use routine terminology and formats that are designed to mirror the experience of taking state tests. Helping children improve their understanding and use of academic language is an essential way to prepare children for assessment. The practice of "teaching to the test" is often criticized—and rightfully so—but helping children understand the language and formats of tests and other assessment instruments levels the playing field for these children, allowing them to demonstrate the skills they've learned, rather than struggling with the test language and formats. All children, but especially English language learners, must be taught test-taking strategies and must build background about the language and procedures of taking tests. **What strategies can you explicitly offer to children to prepare for assessment?**

1. Focus on Academic English and Meaningful Oral Language Experiences

Many English language learners may quickly master *social* English, the conversational language skills and conventions used in everyday interactions with classmates. These same learners, however, frequently encounter difficulty with the *academic* English found on formal assessments. Children may also have gaps in understanding between oral and written English. The structure of academic English is complex, e.g., fiction and nonfiction text structures, paragraph organization, and syntax, including prepositional phrases, introductory clauses, and pronoun references. There are structural analysis constraints at the word, sentence, paragraph, and text levels.

Development of academic language is one of the primary sources of difficulty for English language learners at all ages and grades, while also being fundamental to all children's success. The vocabulary of academic English consists of specialized meanings of common words, abstract concepts, and multiple-meaning words. As children listen to test selections, they may encounter unfamiliar topics and concepts. Recognize that it takes years for children to master academic English, but that you can help them make progress on the way. Highlight and discuss routinely the *academic* language, vocabulary, syntax, and narrative and expository text structures encountered in textbooks and trade books. Remember that academic English is not another name for "standard English." Academic English is the special form of English that is used in the classroom and in written texts. The grammatical constructions, words, and rhetorical conventions are not often used in everyday spoken language. The home language does *not* have to be English in order for children to benefit from experiences in using academic language. If it proves helpful, children may be encouraged to connect what they know in their home languages to what they are learning about academic English.

Provide children with experiences with academic language by reading to them and discussing readings, instructional activities, and experiences. Draw children into instructional conversations focused on the language they encounter in their school texts and other materials to show children how language works. Provide children with ample opportunities to use the language of texts—and tests—in speaking and in writing. Provide regular opportunities for meaningful oral language experiences in which English language learners participate in discussion of important topics and perform the activities required on tests, such as answering comprehension questions, drawing pictures and describing them in a sentence or question, and identifying high-frequency words, parts of speech, and rhyming words. Encourage children to use vocabulary that will support academic language development in increased opportunities for structured academic talk.

2. Focus on Test Directions

Help children understand verbal phrases, such as "draw a circle around," "listen for," or "move down," that are often used in test directions. When possible, model tasks and provide verbal instructions in simpler more common English words. Be explicit in your teaching, using the following examples to guide you.

> **Now I want you to listen for rhyming words.**

For the directions above, talk about the phrase "listen for." Be sure that children understand that they need to *find* the word that rhymes with, or has the same middle and ending sounds as, the key word. Model and gesture how to follow these directions.

> **Yes, *jacks* and *jam* have the same beginning sound.**
> **Draw a circle around the pictures of the *jacks* and the *jam*.**

For the directions above, model and explain how to "draw a circle around" two pictures in a row of three pictures. Be sure that children understand how to do this clearly and neatly.

> **Now move down to the next row where you see the square.**

For the directions above, talk about the phrase "move down." Be sure that children understand that they need to *go to* the *next* row of pictures. Model and gesture how to follow these directions.

3. Focus on Terminology and Strategies

Think about terms that will make the most sense to children as you teach. Instead of using phrases such as "by the square" or "beside the star," for example, you might use more common English phrases, such as *next to the square* or *close to the star* to help children understand what these directions mean.

Preteach the "language of tests" encountered in directions and test items, including:
   Question words, such as: *who, what, which, where, when, why, how,* and *what kind*
   Shape words, such as: *circle, diamond, heart, oval, rectangle, square, star,* and *triangle*
   Place words, such as: *bottom, top, above, below, over, under, up,* and *down*
   Sequence words and phrases, such as: *before, after, first, next, last, then, now, beginning, middle, ending,* and *all day long*

Grammatical words and phrases, such as: *adjective, noun, pronoun, verb, sentence,* and *question*

Descriptive verbs, such as: *look like, feel like, make feel,* and *make happy*

Action verbs, such as: *draw, circle, tell, describe, rhyme, show,* and *write.*

Throughout the year, children need robust vocabulary instruction in English for additional common test words and phrases, such as *blend together, same, different, each, row, picture that shows, sound, telling sentence* or *question, test booklet,* and *form.* Examine the tests for other words and phrases that are important for children to learn.

Familiarize children with basic test formats, such as letter-naming charts, matching charts, and drawing and writing forms, so that they develop skills in locating key information. Use released tests or models of tests, providing children with plenty of practice in test formats, of which there are many at this grade level. Be explicit in your teaching, using the following examples to guide you.

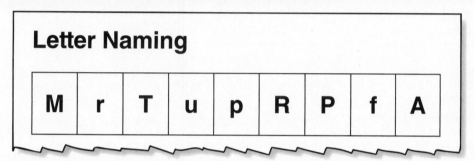

Explain the test format: *Sometimes, tests have many letters. In this test, there are small, lowercase letters and large, uppercase letters. The teacher will point to a letter, and I will tell her the name of that letter, or what that letter is called. The teacher will do that with many letters.* Model and gesture how to use the format.

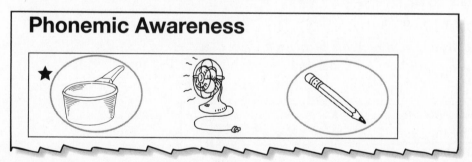

Explain the test format: *Some tests have rows of pictures. There are small, black shapes at the beginning of each row. The teacher will tell me to go to a shape. Put my finger on it. Look at the three pictures next to it. Two words begin with the same sound. One word begins with a different sound. The teacher will ask me to draw a circle around the pictures that begin with the same sound.* Model and gesture how to follow these directions. Be sure that children understand how to do this clearly and neatly.

Writing

Explain the test format: *On this test, there is an empty box and lines to write on. The teacher will ask me to draw a picture in the box. Then she will ask me to write a sentence about it under my picture.* Model and gesture how to follow these directions.

Explain the test format: *The teacher tells me to do one page at a time. This sign is at the bottom of the page. This sign says "Stop." This is the end of the test. I do not turn the page until the teacher tells me.*

Model test-taking strategies for children. Help them use their emerging familiarity with high-frequency words and basic language structures in English to choose the best answer and eliminate incorrect answer choices. The questions in each listening comprehension assessment focus on a particular story element that the children have been taught. Be sure to familiarize children with the various types of listening comprehension questions they may encounter on tests. Use released test items or models of test items to provide children with plenty of practice in various question types and the test-taking strategies you have taught them. Be explicit in your teaching, using the following examples to guide you.

Listening Comprehension

What did Maria's family like to do?
Eat dinner...sing songs...or read books?

Model a test-taking strategy for children—choosing the best answer: *I listened carefully to the whole story. As I listened, I thought about the people in the story. This question asks me to choose the best answer about what Maria's family liked to do. What is the best answer? The answer that matches the story the most. I think about Maria's family in the story. What did they like to do? Sing songs. Now, I look at the three pictures in the row. What do they show? Which picture will I draw a circle around? The picture that shows the family singing. The family likes to eat supper and read books, too, but that is not what this story is mostly about. So, those answers are not the best answer.*

Listening Comprehension

Where did Maria sing?
In her bedroom…at breakfast…or in school?

Model a test-taking strategy for children—eliminating incorrect answer choices: *I listened carefully to the whole story. As I listened, I thought about the people in the story. This question asks about where Maria sang. Where did the story happen? At Maria's home. Now, I look at the three pictures in the row. I think about which answers are not correct. I do not draw a circle around the picture that shows Maria at school. That answer is not correct because the story happens at home. Now I know that the correct answer is one of the other two pictures. The story says that Maria sang at night. So, I do not draw a circle around the picture that shows Maria at breakfast. Breakfast is in the morning, not at night. That picture is not the correct answer. What does the other picture show? It shows that Maria sings by herself in her bedroom. That is the correct answer, so I draw a circle around that picture.*

Summarize test formats and strategies for children. Consider making a T-chart to show examples of the question types that children may find on tests. If your T-chart is large enough to be a wall chart, you can include examples of each type of item from released tests or model tests on the chart. Explain what the structures are and what they ask test-takers to do (or ask children to explain as you teach various strategies).

DIRECTIONS FOR ADMINISTERING UNIT AND END-OF-YEAR BENCHMARK ASSESSMENTS

This section of the manual provides directions for administering each Unit Benchmark Assessment and the End-of-Year Benchmark Assessment. Directions for each assessment begin on the pages listed:

Each Unit Benchmark Assessment and the End-of-Year Benchmark Assessment have different tasks. The directions for each task indicate whether it is designed for administration to an individual, a small group, or the whole class. In many cases, you will be able to choose from two or three of these options in planning how to administer each assessment.

The tasks in these assessments have corresponding pages for children to use in responding to questions. For each task, you will see a reproduction of the test page in the directions (with correct responses indicated, if applicable).

At the end of the directions for each Unit and the End-of-Year Assessment, you will find the **Individual Record** with alignments to Common Core State Standards. You may want to make a copy of the Individual Record for each child and a copy of the **Class Record** (T97) for the whole class to help you record and evaluate the results of each assessment.

Each task in the Unit and End-of-Year Benchmark Assessments is designed to be administered in one sitting of five to ten minutes. You may administer more than one task in one sitting. If a child cannot manage a given task, you may move on to a different task or discontinue the assessment at that point.

In the pages of directions for each assessment, directions printed in **bold** type are intended to be read aloud. Text printed in regular type provides information for your use only.

UNIT 1 DIRECTIONS

1. Letter Naming
(Individual)

Purpose: Assesses ability to recognize uppercase and lowercase letters of the alphabet.

Directions in **bold** are to be read aloud; others are for your information only.

Hand out student page 2. You will ask the child to say the names of the letters as you point to them. Move across the lines from left-to-right as you point to the letters so the child is asked to identify the letters in random order. For some children, it may be necessary to administer the assessment in two sessions. (Note: You may want to make a copy of the page for each child to record his or her performance.)

I will point to a letter and you will tell me the name of that letter.

Scoring: For each child, count the total number of letters correctly named. Using the guidelines below, record each child's score on the Individual Record for the Unit 1 Benchmark Assessment (T25).

Number Correct	Rating	
All	Proficient	+
45 – 51	Developing	✓
Less than 45	Emerging	–

Letter Naming

M	r	T	u	p	R	P	f	A
S	G	b	E	K	o	w	n	Z
y	a	W	N	L	e	d	h	s
V	q	O	i	z	U	g	m	v
D	c	X	J	F	Q	j	x	C
H	k	B	l	Y	I	t		

STOP

2   Benchmark Assessment Unit 1

2. Phonological Awareness: Rhyming
(Individual or small group)

Purpose: Assesses ability to recognize rhyme.

Hand out student page 3. Use the following directions to administer the assessment, beginning with the sample question. Children are to respond by circling the answer to each question. If children are unfamiliar with circling answers, write three words in a row on the chalkboard and demonstrate how to draw a circle around one of the words.

Now I want you to listen for rhyming words. Let's do the first one together. Find the small star at the top of the page. Put your finger on it. Now look at the picture by the star. It is a *boat*. Say the word. (boat) Look at the three pictures in the same row: *cat, coat, boy*. Which word rhymes with *boat—cat, coat,* or *boy*? (Pause.) Yes, *coat* rhymes with *boat*. Draw a circle around the picture of the *coat* because *coat* is the word that rhymes with *boat*.

When you are sure that each child understands the task and has followed the directions for completing the sample item, administer each test item.

1. **Now move down to the next row where you see the square. Put your finger on it. Look at the picture by the square. It is a *rake*. Look at the three pictures in the same row: *sock, rug, cake*. Draw a circle around the word that rhymes with *rake . . . rake*.**

2. **Move down to the next row, the circle, where you see the *dish*. Look at the pictures: *desk, fish, brush*. Draw a circle around the word that rhymes with *dish . . . dish*.**

3. **Move down to the next row, the triangle, where you see the *clock*. Look at the pictures: *duck, clown, rock*. Draw a circle around the word that rhymes with *clock . . . clock*.**

4. **Move down to the last row, the heart, where you see the *bone*. Look at the pictures: *phone, bean, mouse*. Draw a circle around the word that rhymes with *bone . . . bone*.**

- - - Phonological Awareness: Rhyming - - -

Scoring: For each child, mark the answer to each question correct or incorrect. Then count the total number correct for each child. Using the guidelines below, record the child's score on the Individual Record for the Unit 1 Benchmark Assessment (T25).

Number Correct	Rating	
4	Proficient	+
3	Developing	✓
Less than 3	Emerging	–

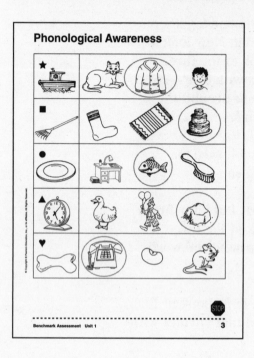

3. Word Knowledge: High-Frequency Words

(Individual or small group)

Purpose: Assesses ability to recognize high-frequency words.

Hand out student page 4. Use the following directions to administer the assessment. If necessary, demonstrate on the chalkboard how to draw a line from a picture to its matching word.

Move through the assessment quickly to be sure you are assessing the child's ability to recognize high-frequency words quickly.

Let's find some words you know.

1. **Find the picture of the star. Put your finger on it. Now look at the words on the page. Find the word *little*. Draw a line from the star to the word *little*.**

2. **Move down to the picture of the bird. Put your finger on it. Now find the word *I*. Draw a line from the bird to the word *I*.**

3. **Move down to the picture of the dog. Put your finger on it. Now find the word *to*. Draw a line from the dog to the word *to*.**

4. **Move down to the picture of the fish. Put your finger on it. Now find the word *am*. Draw a line from the fish to the word *am*.**

5. **Move down to the picture of the cat. Put your finger on it. Now find the word *the*. Draw a line from the cat to the word *the*.**

6. **Move down to the picture of the horse. Put your finger on it. Now find the word *a*. Draw a line from the horse to the word *a*.**

Scoring: For each child, count the total number of words matched correctly. Using the guidelines below, record the child's score on the Individual Record for the Unit 1 Benchmark Assessment (T25).

Number Correct	Rating	
6	Proficient	+
4 – 5	Developing	✓
Less than 4	Emerging	–

Word Knowledge

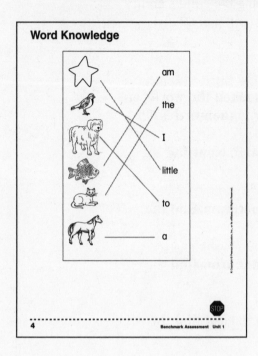

4. Listening Comprehension: Character

(Individual or small group)

Purpose: Assesses general comprehension.

Hand out student page 5. Read the story aloud. Then read each question that follows. Children are to respond by circling the answer to each question. If children are unfamiliar with circling answers, draw three simple pictures in a row on the chalkboard and demonstrate how to draw a circle around one of the pictures.

I am going to read a story about a girl named Maria. Then I will ask you some questions. Listen carefully. Here is the story.

Everyone in Maria's family loved to sing. They sang all the time. Maria's mom sang while she cooked dinner. Her dad sang while he washed the dishes. And her sister sang while she swept the floor. Maria sang too, but only when no one could hear her. She thought she did not sing well.

"Maria, sing with us," begged her dad every night after dinner. He started to sing her favorite song. Everyone joined in—except Maria.

But later, when Maria was alone in her bedroom, she did what she did every night. She sat by her window and sang. Her voice drifted out into the warm night air.

The next morning as Maria walked past the house next door, she heard someone singing her favorite song. Just then her neighbor Mr. Suarez opened the door and came outside.

"It's a beautiful day, isn't it?" he said to Maria.

"Yes it is," Maria answered. "But the day is not as beautiful as the voice that I hear coming from your house. Who is that singing?"

"That's my pet parrot," said Mr. Suarez.

"Your parrot," said Maria in surprise. "But how did your parrot learn to sing that song?"

"He learned it from you," answered Mr. Suarez. "We listen to you sing every night. He is singing in your voice. You're the one with the beautiful voice."

That night Maria finally sang along with her family.

Now I am going to ask you some questions about the story. For each question that I ask, there are three pictures. Draw a circle around the picture that shows the best answer. Listen carefully.

1. Look at the first row of pictures at the top of the page where you see the square. Put your finger on the square. What did Maria's family like to do? *Eat dinner . . . sing songs . . . or read books?* Draw a circle around the picture that shows the best answer.

2. Move down to the next row of pictures where you see the circle. Put your finger on the circle. How did Maria feel about her singing at the beginning of the story? *Bad . . . proud . . . or scared?* Draw a circle around the picture that shows how she felt about her singing at the beginning of the story.

3. Move down to the next row of pictures where you see the triangle. Put your finger on the triangle. Where did Maria sing? *In her bedroom . . . at breakfast . . . or in school?* Draw a circle around the picture that shows where Maria sang.

4. Move down to the next row of pictures where you see the heart. Put your finger on the heart. Who heard Maria singing every night? *Her parents . . . her friends . . . or Mr. Suarez?* Draw a circle around the picture that shows who heard Maria singing every night.

5. Move down to the next row of pictures where you see the rectangle. Put your finger on the rectangle. How did Maria feel when she found out that a parrot was singing? *Sad . . . surprised . . . or mad?* Draw a circle around the picture that shows how she felt.

Scoring: For each child, mark the answer to each question correct or incorrect. Then count the total number correct for each child. Using the guidelines below, record the child's score on the Individual Record for the Unit 1 Benchmark Assessment (T25).

Number Correct	Rating	
5	Proficient	+
3 – 4	Developing	✓
Less than 3	Emerging	–

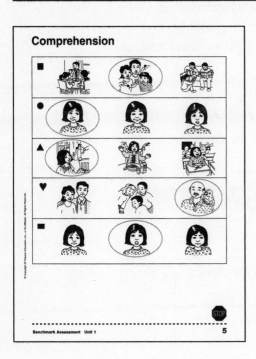

5. Writing: Nouns
(Individual, small group, or whole class)

Purpose: Assesses ability to draw a person, animal, place, or thing and write a sentence about it.

Hand out student page 6. Children will draw a picture of a noun and write a sentence about it. If the child is unable to write the sentence, have him or her dictate the sentence to you. Record the sentence on the page under the picture.

Now we are going to do something different. Look at the picture frame on your page. You are going to draw a picture of a noun. Remember that a noun is a person, animal, place, or thing. Draw a picture of a noun you like. Then write a sentence that tells about your picture.

Scoring: After children complete their work, place a checkmark beside each attribute the child has included in the drawing and the writing. Using the guidelines below, evaluate the child's work and record the child's score on the Individual Record for the Unit 1 Benchmark Assessment (T25).

Scoring Guidelines	Rating	
The child draws a recognizable person, animal, place, or thing and writes a sentence that tells about the picture.	Proficient	+
The child draws a reasonable picture and writes some words or dictates a sentence.	Developing	✓
The child attempts to draw a picture and attempts to write or dictate a sentence, but both are less than complete and correct.	Emerging	–

Writing

STOP

6   Benchmark Assessment Unit 1

INDIVIDUAL RECORD

Unit 1 Benchmark Assessment

Child's Name _____ **Date** _____

Directions: Record the results of the Unit 1 Benchmark Assessment by marking Proficient (+), Developing (✓), or Emerging (–) beside each assessed skill.

Unit 1 Assessed Skills	Proficient (+)	Developing (✓)	Emerging (–)	Common Core State Standard
Letter Naming				Foundational Skills 1.d.
Phonological Awareness: Rhyming				Foundational Skills 2.a.
Word Knowledge: High-Frequency Words				Foundational Skills 3.c.
Listening Comprehension: Character				Literature 3.
Writing: Nouns				Writing 2.

Notes/Observations

UNIT 2 DIRECTIONS

1. Phonemic Awareness: Initial Sounds (/m/, /t/, short **a**, /s/, /p/, /k/ spelled **c**, short **i**)

(Individual or small group)

Purpose: Assesses ability to recognize initial sounds.

Directions in **bold** are to be read aloud; others are for your information only.

Hand out student pages 2 and 3. Use the following directions to administer the test, beginning with the sample question.

We are going to listen for the beginning sound in a word. Listen carefully. Let's do the first one together. Find the small star at the top of the page. Put your finger on it. Now look at the three pictures in the row beside the star: *pot, fan, pencil*. Listen to the beginning sound of each word: *pot, fan, pencil*. Two of the words begin with the same sound. One of the words begins with a different sound. Which two words have the same beginning sound? (Pause.) **Yes, *pot* and *pencil* have the same beginning sound. Draw a circle around the pictures of the *pot* and the *pencil* because they begin with the same sound.**

When you are sure that each child understands the task and has followed the directions for completing the sample item, administer each test item.

1. **Move down to the next row where you see the square. Put your finger on the square. Look at the three pictures in the same row: *moon, mop, house*. Draw a circle around the two pictures that have the same sound at the beginning: *moon . . . mop . . . house*.**

2. **Move down to the next row where you see the circle. Put your finger on the circle. Look at the pictures: *ball, table, tire*. Draw a circle around the two pictures that have the same sound at the beginning: *ball . . . table . . . tire*.**

3. **Move down to the next row where you see the triangle. Put your finger on the triangle. Look at the pictures: *apple, umbrella, ant*. Draw a circle around the two pictures that have the same beginning sound: *apple . . . umbrella . . . ant*.**

4. **Move down to the next row where you see the heart. Put your finger on the heart. Look at the pictures in the row: *sun, soap, cake*. Draw a circle around the two pictures that have the same beginning sound: *sun . . . soap . . . cake*.**

5. **Now look at the next page. Go to the first row where you see the square. Put your finger on the square. Look at the pictures in the row: *rake, pig, pond*. Draw a circle around the two pictures that have the same beginning sound: *rake . . . pig . . . pond*.**

6. **Move down to the next row where you see the circle. Put your finger on the circle. Look at the pictures in the row:** *cat, foot, cup.* **Draw a circle around the two pictures that have the same beginning sound:** *cat . . . foot . . . cup.*

7. **Move down to the last row where you see the triangle. Put your finger on the triangle. Look at the pictures in the row:** *igloo, inch, octopus.* **Draw a circle around the two pictures that have the same beginning sound:** *igloo . . . inch . . . octopus.*

Scoring: For each child, mark the answer to each question correct or incorrect. Then count the total number correct for each child. Using the guidelines below, record the child's score on the Individual Record for the Unit 2 Benchmark Assessment (T35).

Number Correct	Rating	
7	Proficient	+
5 – 6	Developing	✓
Less than 5	Emerging	−

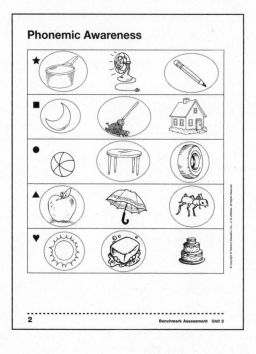

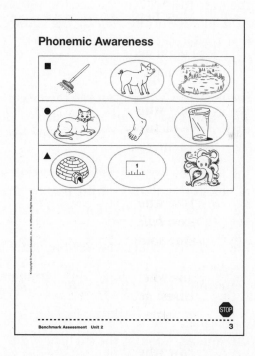

2. Phonics: Letter-Sound Correspondence (*m*, *t*, short *a*, *s*, *p*, *c*, short *i*)

(Individual or small group)

Purpose: Assesses ability to connect sound to letter.

Hand out student pages 4 and 5. Use the following directions to administer the assessment, beginning with the sample question.

Now we are going to find the letter for a sound. Let's do the first one together. Find the small star at the top of the page. Put your finger on it. Now look at the picture by the star. It is a *pin*. The middle sound in *pin* is /i/. Now look at the letters in the row next to the picture. Which is the letter for /i/? (Pause.) **Yes, the last letter in the row is the letter for /i/. Draw a circle around the letter for /i/.**

When you are sure that each child understands the task and has followed the directions for completing the sample item, administer each test item.

1. **Move down to the next row where you see the square. Put your finger on the square. Look at the picture of the *map* by the square. The first sound in *map* is /m/. Now look at the letters in the row next to the picture. What is the letter for /m/? Circle the letter for /m/.**

2. **Move down to the next row where you see the circle. Put your finger on the circle. Look at the picture of the *top* by the circle. The first sound in *top* is /t/. What is the letter for /t/? Circle the letter for /t/.**

3. **Move down to the next row where you see the triangle. Put your finger on the triangle. Look at the picture of the *mat* by the triangle. The middle sound in *mat* is /a/. What is the letter for /a/? Circle the letter for /a/.**

4. **Move down to the next row where you see the heart. Put your finger on the heart. Look at the picture of the *sock* by the heart. The first sound in *sock* is /s/. What is the letter for /s/? Circle the letter for /s/.**

5. **Now look at the next page. Go to the first row where you see the square. Put your finger on the square. Look at the picture of the *pan* by the square. The first sound in *pan* is /p/. What is the letter for /p/? Circle the letter for /p/.**

6. **Move down to the next row where you see the circle. Put your finger on the circle. Look at the picture of the *car* by the circle. The first sound in *car* is /k/. What is the letter for /k/? Circle the letter for /k/.**

7. **Move down to the last row where you see the triangle. Put your finger on the triangle. Look at the picture of the *fin* of the fish by the triangle. The middle sound in *fin* is /i/. What is the letter for /i/? Circle the letter for /i/.**

Scoring: For each child, mark the answer to each question correct or incorrect. Then count the total number correct for each child. Using the guidelines below, record the child's score on the Individual Record for the Unit 2 Benchmark Assessment (T35).

Number Correct	Rating	
7	Proficient	+
5 – 6	Developing	✓
Less than 5	Emerging	–

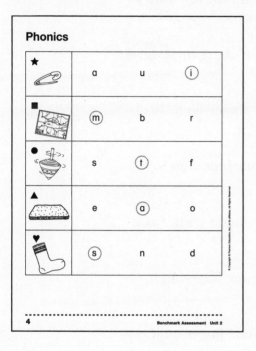

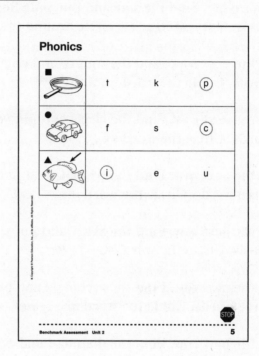

3. Word Knowledge: High-Frequency Words

(Individual or small group)

Purpose: Assesses ability to recognize high-frequency words.

Hand out student page 6. As you say a word aloud, the child will circle it. Move through the assessment quickly to make sure you are assessing the child's ability to recognize the high-frequency words quickly.

1. **Now I am going to say one word in each row, and you are going to circle the word that I am saying. Find the star and put your finger on it. Now look at the three words in that row. Draw a circle around the word** *have . . . have.*

2. **Move down to the next row. Find the square and put your finger on it. Look at the three words. Circle the word** *is . . . is.*

3. **Move down to the next row. Find the circle and put your finger on it. Look at the three words. Circle the word** *we . . . we.*

4. **Move down to the next row. Find the triangle and put your finger on it. Look at the three words. Circle the word** *my . . . my.*

5. **Move down to the next row. Find the heart and put your finger on it. Look at the three words. Circle the word** *like . . . like.*

6. **Move down to the next row. Find the rectangle and put your finger on it. Look at the three words. Circle the word** *he . . . he.*

7. **Move down to the next row. Find the diamond and put your finger on it. Look at the three words. Circle the word** *for . . . for.*

Scoring: For each child, mark the answer to each question correct or incorrect. Then count the total number of words circled correctly. Using the guidelines below, record the child's score on the Individual Record for the Unit 2 Benchmark Assessment (T35).

Number Correct	Rating	
7	Proficient	+
5 – 6	Developing	✓
Less than 5	Emerging	–

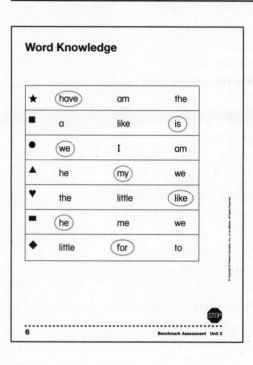

4. Listening Comprehension: Setting

(Individual, small group, or whole class)

Purpose: Assesses general comprehension.

Hand out student page 7. Read the story aloud. Then read each question that follows. Children will circle the answer to each question. Pause after each question to allow time for children to mark their answers.

Now I am going to read a story about a boy named Michael. Then I will ask you some questions. Listen carefully. Here is the story.

Michael turned on the radio. He wanted to hear the weather report.

"You don't need the weatherman," said his father. "Just look outside."

Michael looked out the window. Everything was covered with snow, and it was still snowing.

Michael sighed. Now he wouldn't be able to go to his friend Peter's house to spend the night. The heavy snow was making it dangerous to drive.

"We can walk to Peter's house in about twenty minutes even in this snow," said Michael's father. "We can use your sled to carry your stuff. Let's go!"

Michael hurried to get his backpack. Then he and his father put on their winter jackets, hats, boots, and gloves. They tied Michael's backpack to the sled and dragged the sled out of the garage.

The streets were silent. Even though it was nighttime, everything looked bright because of the snow. Michael and his father walked quietly. They took turns pulling the sled.

Twenty minutes later they arrived at Peter's house and knocked on the door. Peter started to laugh as soon as he opened the door. "You two look like snowmen," he said.

"Then we won't have to build one," Michael said.

But of course the boys did build a snowman—right after breakfast the next morning.

Now I am going to ask you some questions about the story. For each question that I ask, there are three pictures in a row. Draw a circle around the picture that shows the best answer. Listen carefully.

1. **Look at the first row of pictures at the top of the page where there is a square. Put your finger on the square. What was the weather like in this story?** *Sunny . . . snowy . . . or rainy?* **Draw a circle around the picture that shows what the weather was like.**

2. **Move down to the next row of pictures where you see the circle. Put your finger on the circle. What did Michael put on his feet before he went to Peter's house?** *Sandals . . . sneakers . . . or boots?* **Draw a circle around the picture that shows what Michael put on his feet.**

Listening Comprehension: Setting

3. **Move down to the next row where you see the triangle. Put your finger on the triangle. Where did Michael put his backpack?** *On a sled . . . in the car . . . or in the closet?* **Draw a circle around the picture that shows where Michael put his backpack.**

4. **Move down to the next row where you see the heart. Put your finger on the heart. How did Michael get to Peter's house?** *By car . . . by walking . . . or by skating?* **Draw a circle around the picture that shows how Michael got to Peter's house.**

5. **Move down to the last row where you see the rectangle. Put your finger on the rectangle. When did this story happen?** *In the morning . . . at lunchtime . . . or at night?* **Draw a circle around the picture that shows when the story happened.**

Scoring: For each child, mark the answer to each question correct or incorrect. Then count the total number correct for each child. Using the guidelines below, record the child's score on the Individual Record for the Unit 2 Benchmark Assessment (T35).

Number Correct	Rating	
5	Proficient	+
3 – 4	Developing	✓
Less than 3	Emerging	–

5. Writing: Adjectives
(Individual, small group, or whole class)

Purpose: Assesses ability to draw a picture and write a sentence that uses an adjective to describe the picture.

Hand out student page 8. Children will draw a picture and write a sentence with an adjective that describes the picture. If the child is not able to write the sentence, have him or her dictate it to you. Record the sentence under the picture.

Remember that adjectives are words that describe people, animals, places, and things, such as their color, size, shape, and number. Adjectives can describe opposites also. Draw a picture of something that you like. Then write a sentence about your picture that uses one or two adjectives.

Scoring: Using the guidelines below, evaluate the child's work and record the child's score on the Individual Record for the Unit 2 Benchmark Assessment (T35).

Scoring Guidelines	Rating	
The child draws a recognizable picture and writes a sentence using an appropriate adjective or adjectives to describe the picture.	Proficient	+
The child draws a reasonable picture and writes some words or dictates a sentence that describes the picture.	Developing	✓
The child draws a picture and attempts to write or dictate a sentence to describe it, but both are less than complete and correct.	Emerging	–

Writing

INDIVIDUAL RECORD

Unit 2 Benchmark Assessment

Child's Name _____ **Date** _____

Directions: Record the results of the Unit 2 Benchmark Assessment by marking Proficient (+), Developing (✓), or Emerging (–) beside each assessed skill.

Unit 2 Assessed Skills	Proficient (+)	Developing (✓)	Emerging (–)	Common Core State Standard
Phonemic Awareness: Initial Sounds (/m/, /t/, short *a*, /s/, /p/, /k/ spelled *c*, short *i*)				Foundational Skills 2.d.
Phonics: Letter-Sound Correspondence (*m, t*, short *a, s, p, c,* short *i*)				Foundational Skills 3.a., 3.b.
Word Knowledge: High-Frequency Words				Foundational Skills 3.c.
Listening Comprehension: Setting				Literature 3.
Writing: Adjectives				Writing 2.

Notes/Observations

UNIT 3 DIRECTIONS

1. Phonemic Awareness: Initial Sounds (/b/, /n/, /r/, /d/, /k/, /f/, short *o*)
(Individual or small group)

Purpose: Assesses ability to recognize initial sounds.

Directions in **bold** are to be read aloud; others are for your information only.

Hand out student pages 2 and 3. Use the following directions to administer the test, beginning with the sample question.

Now we are going to listen to the beginning sound of a word. Let's do the first one together. Find the small star at the top of the page. Put your finger on it. Now look at the picture by the star. It is a *fish*. The beginning sound in *fish* is /f/. Now look at the three pictures in the same row: *bird, house, foot*. Which word begins with the same sound as *fish—bird, house,* or *foot*? (Pause.) **Yes, *foot* starts with the same sound as *fish*. Draw a circle around the picture of the foot because *foot* is the word that begins with the same sound as *fish*.**

When you are sure that each child understands the task and has followed the directions for completing the sample item, administer each test item.

1. **Move down to the next row where you see the picture of a *book* by the square. Put your finger on the square. Look at the pictures in the same row: *bag, gate, pen*. Circle the word that begins with the same sound as *book . . . book*.**

2. **Move down to the next row where you see the picture of the *nest* by the circle. Put your finger on the circle. Look at the pictures in the same row: *mouse, top, nose*. Circle the word that begins with the same sound as *nest . . . nest*.**

3. **Move down to the next row where you see the picture of the *rake* by the triangle. Put your finger on the triangle. Look at the pictures in the same row: *cat, rose, bean*. Circle the word that begins with the same sound as *rake . . . rake*.**

4. **Move down to the next row where you see the picture of the *deer* by the heart. Put your finger on the heart. Look at the pictures in the same row: *pig, desk, box*. Circle the word that begins with the same sound as *deer . . . deer*.**

5. **Now look at the next page. Go to the first row where you see the picture of the *kite* by the square. Put your finger on the square. Look at the pictures in the same row: *key, bell, goat*. Circle the word that begins with the same sound as *kite . . . kite*.**

6. **Move down to the next row where you see the picture of the *fork* by the circle. Put your finger on the circle. Look at the pictures in the same row: *fence, leaf, pail.* Circle the word that begins with the same sound as *fork . . . fork.***

7. **Move down to the last row where you see the picture of the *ox* by the triangle. Put your finger on the triangle. Look at the pictures in the same row: *ape, octopus, eagle.* Circle the word that begins with the same sound as *ox . . . ox.***

Scoring: For each child, mark the answer to each question correct or incorrect. Then count the total number correct for each child. Using the guidelines below, record the child's score on the Individual Record for the Unit 3 Benchmark Assessment (T45).

Number Correct	Rating	
7	Proficient	+
5 – 6	Developing	✓
Less than 5	Emerging	–

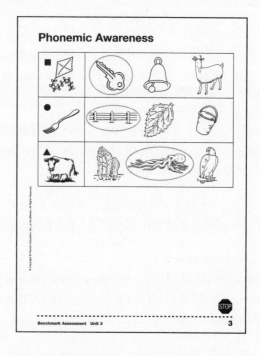

2. Phonics: Letter-Sound Correspondence (**b, n, r, d, k, f, short o**)

(Individual or small group)

Purpose: Assesses ability to connect sound to letter.

Hand out student pages 4 and 5. Use the following directions to administer the assessment, beginning with the sample question.

Now we are going to find the letter for a sound. Let's do the first one together. Find the small star at the top of the page. Put your finger on it. Now look at the picture by the star. It is a picture of a *mat*. The first sound in *mat* is /m/. Now look at the letters in the same row. What is the letter for /m/? (Pause) **Yes, the first letter in the row is the letter for /m/. Draw a circle around the letter *m*.**

When you are sure that each child understands the task and has followed the directions for completing the sample item, administer each test item.

1. **Move down to the next row where you see the square. Put your finger on the square. Look at the picture of the *bed*. The first sound in *bed* is /b/. What is the letter for /b/? Circle the letter for /b/.**

2. **Move down to the next row where you see the circle. Put your finger on the circle. Look at the picture of the *nail*. The first sound in *nail* is /n/. What is the letter for /n/? Circle the letter for /n/.**

3. **Move down to the next row where you see the triangle. Put your finger on the triangle. Look at the picture of the *rabbit*. The first sound in *rabbit* is /r/. What is the letter for /r/? Circle the letter for /r/.**

4. **Move down to the next row where you see the heart. Put your finger on the heart. Look at the picture of the *dog*. The first sound in *dog* is /d/. What is the letter for /d/? Circle the letter for /d/.**

5. **Now look at the next page. Go to the first row where you see the square. Put your finger on the square. Look at the picture of the *kite*. The first sound in *kite* is /k/. What is the letter for /k/? Circle the letter for /k/.**

6. **Move down to the next row where you see the circle. Put your finger on the circle. Look at the picture of the *fan*. The first sound in *fan* is /f/. What is the letter for /f/? Circle the letter for /f/.**

7. **Move down to the last row where you see the triangle. Put your finger on the triangle. Look at the picture of the *pot*. The middle sound in *pot* is /o/. What is the letter for /o/? Circle the letter for /o/.**

Scoring: For each child, mark the answer to each question correct or incorrect. Then count the total number correct for each child. Using the guidelines below, record the child's score on the Individual Record for the Unit 3 Benchmark Assessment (T45).

Number Correct	Rating	
7	Proficient	+
5 – 6	Developing	✓
Less than 5	Emerging	–

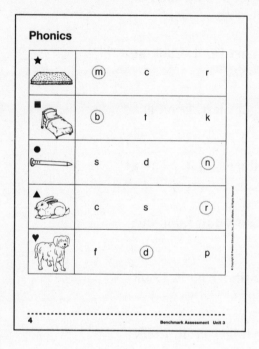

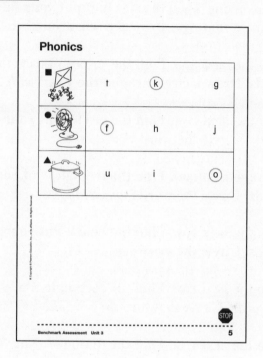

3. Word Knowledge: High-Frequency Words

(Individual or small group)

Purpose: Assesses ability to recognize high-frequency words.

Hand out student page 6. As you say a word aloud, the child will circle it. Move through the assessment quickly to make sure you are assessing the child's ability to recognize the high-frequency words quickly.

1. **Now I am going to say one word in each row, and you are going to circle the word that I am saying. Find the star and put your finger on it. Now look at the three words in that row. Draw a circle around the word** *me . . . me.*

2. **Move down to the next row. Find the square. Put your finger on it. Look at the three words. Draw a circle around the word** *with . . . with.*

3. **Move down to the next row. Find the circle. Put your finger on it. Look at the three words. Circle the word** *she . . . she.*

4. **Move down to the next row. Find the triangle. Put your finger on it. Look at the three words. Circle the word** *look . . . look.*

5. **Move down to the next row. Find the heart. Put your finger on it. Look at the three words. Circle the word** *see . . . see.*

6. **Move down to the next row. Find the rectangle. Put your finger on it. Look at the three words. Circle the word** *they . . . they.*

7. **Move down to the next row. Find the diamond. Put your finger on it. Look at the three words. Circle the word** *you . . . you.*

8. **Move down to the next row. Find the oval. Put your finger on it. Look at the three words. Circle the word** *of . . . of.*

Scoring: For each child, count the total number of words circled correctly. Using the guidelines below, record the child's score on the Individual Record for the Unit 3 Benchmark Assessment (T45).

Number Correct	Rating	
8	Proficient	+
5 – 7	Developing	✓
Less than 5	Emerging	–

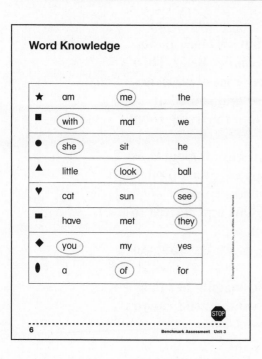

4. Listening Comprehension: Main Idea
(Individual, small group, or whole class)

Purpose: Assesses general comprehension.

Hand out student page 7. Read the story aloud. Then read each question that follows. Have children respond by circling the answer to each question.

Now I am going to read a story about a girl named Shari. Then I will ask you some questions. Listen carefully. Here is the story.

> Shari was getting ready for the school play. First, she put on black pants and a black shirt. Next, she put a pair of pointy black ears on her head. Then she pinned a long black tail to her pants. Finally, she pasted a set of whiskers on her cheeks. When she was done, she looked in the mirror and smiled at herself. She was ready. She let out a loud meow and crept into the living room on her hands and knees.
>
> Shari's family was waiting to see what she looked like. They all giggled as she meowed and meowed. But Jake the dog barked and barked. Shari thought that was strange. Jake never barked at her. Why was he barking now?
>
> Next Jake did something even stranger. He ran up to Shari and started to tug on her tail. Shari's father rescued the tail from Jake's mouth.
>
> "Stand up, Shari," said her father. "Jake thinks you're a cat. He wants to chase you."
>
> Shari stood up. Sure enough, Jake stopped barking and tugging her tail.
>
> "Well," said Shari's mother with a laugh, "that shows what a good cat you are. You're certainly ready for the school play."

Now I am going to ask you some questions about the story. For each question there are three pictures in a row. Draw a circle around the picture that shows the best answer. Listen carefully.

1. **Look at the first row of pictures at the top of the page where you see the square. Put your finger on the square. What kind of animal did Shari pretend to be? Draw a circle around the picture that shows what kind of animal Shari pretended to be.**

2. **Move down to the next row of pictures where you see the circle. Put your finger on the circle. What did Shari's family do when she meowed and meowed? Draw a circle that shows what Shari's family did when she meowed and meowed.**

3. **Move down to the next row of pictures where you see the triangle. Put your finger on the triangle. What did Jake the dog do when he saw Shari? Draw a circle around the picture that shows what Jake the dog did when he saw Shari.**

4. **Move down to the next row of pictures where you see the heart. Put your finger on the heart. How did Shari's dad help her? Draw a circle around the picture that shows what Shari's dad did to help her.**

5. Move down to the last row of pictures where you see the rectangle. Put your finger on the rectangle. Who told Shari to stand up? Draw a circle around the picture that shows who told Shari to stand up.

Scoring: For each child, mark the answer to each question correct or incorrect. Then count the total number correct for each child. Using the guidelines below, record the child's score on the Individual Record for the Unit 3 Benchmark Assessment (T45).

Number Correct	Rating	
5	Proficient	+
3 – 4	Developing	✓
Less than 3	Emerging	–

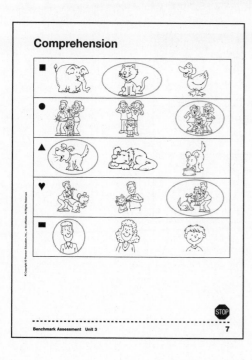

5. Writing: Verbs

(Individual, small group, or whole class)

Purpose: Assesses ability to write a sentence using a verb.

Hand out student page 8. Children will draw a picture and, underneath it, write a sentence using an action verb. If the child is unable to write the sentence, have him or her dictate the sentence to you. Record the sentence under the picture.

Remember that a verb is an action word that tells about things we do. Draw a picture of yourself or an animal doing something. Then write a sentence about what is happening in your picture.

Scoring: Using the guidelines below, evaluate the child's work and record the child's score on the Individual Record for the Unit 3 Benchmark Assessment (T45).

Scoring Guidelines	Rating	
The child draws a recognizable picture and writes a sentence using a verb to describe the picture.	Proficient	+
The child draws a reasonable picture and writes some words or dictates a sentence that uses a verb.	Developing	✓
The child draws a picture and attempts to write or dictate a sentence using a verb, but both are less than complete and correct.	Emerging	−

Writing

STOP

8   Benchmark Assessment Unit 3

INDIVIDUAL RECORD

Unit 3 Benchmark Assessment

Child's Name _____ **Date** _____

Directions: Record the results of the Unit 3 Benchmark Assessment by marking Proficient (+), Developing (✓), or Emerging (–) beside each assessed skill.

Unit 3 Assessed Skills	Proficient (+)	Developing (✓)	Emerging (–)	Common Core State Standard
Phonemic Awareness: Initial Sounds (/b/, /n/, /r/, /d/, /k/, /f/, short *o*)				Foundational Skills 2.d.
Phonics: Letter-Sound Correspondence (*b, n, r, d, k, f,* short *o*)				Foundational Skills 3.a., 3.b.
Word Knowledge: High-Frequency Words				Foundational Skills 3.c.
Listening Comprehension: Main Idea				Informational Text 2.
Writing: Verbs				Writing 3.

Notes/Observations

UNIT 4 DIRECTIONS

1. Phonemic Awareness: Recognizing Initial and Final Sounds

(Individual or small group)

Purpose: Assesses ability to recognize initial and final sounds, including some consonant blends.

Hand out student pages 2–3. Use the following directions to administer the test, beginning with the sample question. Directions in **bold** are to be read aloud. The others are for your information only.

Now you are going to listen to sounds in words. Let's do the first one together. Find the small star. Put your finger on it. Now look at the three pictures in the row beside the star: *heart, hand, shirt*. Listen to the beginning sound of each word: *heart, hand, shirt*. Two of the words begin with the same sound. One of the words begins with a different sound. Which two words have the same beginning sound? (Pause.) **Yes, *heart* and *hand* have the same beginning sound. Draw a circle around the pictures of the *heart* and the *hand*.**

When you are sure that each child understands the task and has followed the directions for completing the sample item, administer each test item.

1. **Move down to the next row where you see the square. Put your finger on the square. Now look at the pictures in the same row: *tree, car, truck*. Circle the pictures that have the same sound at the beginning: *tree . . . car . . . truck*.**

2. **Move down to the next row where you see the circle. Put your finger on the circle. Look at the pictures: *elephant, egg, ox*. Circle the pictures that have the same sound at the beginning: *elephant . . . egg . . . ox*.**

3. **Move down to the next row where you see the triangle. Put your finger on the triangle. Look at the pictures: *spoon, bread, spider*. Circle the pictures that have the same sound at the beginning: *spoon . . . bread . . . spider*.**

4. **Move down to the next row where you see the heart. Put your finger on the heart. Look at the pictures: *broom, drum, dress*. Circle the pictures that have the same sound at the beginning: *broom . . . drum . . . dress*.**

5. **Go to the top of the next page. Look at the top row where you see the square. Put your finger on the square. Look at the pictures: *hat, goat, house*. Circle the pictures that have the same sound at the beginning: *hat . . . goat . . . house*.**

6. **Move down to the next row where you see the circle. Put your finger on the circle. Look at the pictures. Listen for the ending sound: *rake, ball, nail*. Circle the pictures that have the same sound at the end: *rake . . . ball . . . nail*.**

7. **Move down to the next row where you see the triangle. Put your finger on the triangle. Look at the pictures. Listen for the ending sound:** *bag, pig, cup.* **Circle the pictures that have the same sound at the end:** *bag . . . pig . . . cup.*

8. **Move down to the last row where you see the heart. Put your finger on the heart. Look at the pictures. Listen for the ending sound:** *nest, milk, fist.* **Circle the pictures that have the same sound at the end:** *nest . . . milk . . . fist.*

Scoring: For each child, mark the answer to each question correct or incorrect. Then count the total number correct for each child. Using the guidelines below, record the child's score on the Individual Record for the Unit 4 Benchmark Assessment (T57).

Number Correct	Rating	
8	Proficient	+
6 – 7	Developing	✓
Less than 6	Emerging	–

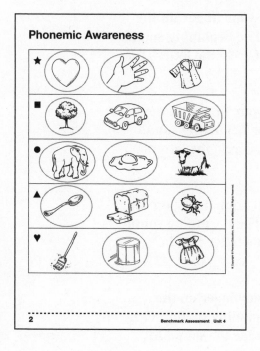

2. Phonics: Letter-Sound Correspondence (*h, l, g, short e, st-, sp-, tr-, bl-, br-, dr-, -st, -sp, -lk*)
(Individual or small group)

Purpose: Assesses ability to connect sound to letter.

Hand out student pages 4–5. Use the following directions to administer the assessment, beginning with the sample question.

Now we are going to find letters for a sound. Let's do the first one together. Find the small star. Put your finger on it. Now look at the picture by the star. It is a picture of a *tree*. The beginning sound in *tree* is /tr/. Now look at the letters in the same row. Which are the letters for the sound /tr/? (Pause.) **Yes, the last two letters in the row are the letters for the sound /tr/. Draw a circle around the letters *tr* because those are the letters for the sound /tr/.**

When you are sure that each child understands the task and has followed the directions for completing the sample item, administer each test item.

1. **Move down to the next row where you see a square. Put your finger on the square. Look at the picture of the *spoon* by the square. The beginning sound in *spoon* is /sp/. What are the letters for the sound /sp/? Circle the letters for the sound /sp/.**

2. **Move down to the next row where you see a circle. Put your finger on the circle. Look at the picture of the *broom* by the circle. The beginning sound in *broom* is /br/. What are the letters for the sound /br/? Circle the letters for the sound /br/.**

3. **Move down to the next row where you see a triangle. Put your finger on the triangle. Look at the picture of the *leaf* by the triangle. The beginning sound in *leaf* is /l/. What is the letter for the sound /l/? Circle the letter for the sound /l/.**

4. **Move down to the next row where you see a heart. Put your finger on the heart. Look at the picture of the *egg* by the heart. The beginning sound in *egg* is /e/. What is the letter for the sound /e/? Circle the letter for the sound /e/.**

5. **Turn to the next page. Look at the top row where you see a square. Put your finger on the square. Look at the picture of the *house* by the square. The beginning sound in *house* is /h/. What is the letter for the sound /h/? Circle the letter for the sound /h/.**

6. **Move down to the next row where you see a circle. Put your finger on the circle. Look at the picture of the *dog* by the circle. The ending sound in *dog* is /g/. What is the letter for the sound /g/? Circle the letter for the sound /g/.**

7. **Move down to the next row where you see a triangle. Put your finger on the triangle. Look at the picture of** *milk* **by the triangle. The ending sound in** *milk* **is /lk/. What are the letters for the sound /lk/? Circle the letters for the sound /lk/.**

8. **Move down to the last row where you see a heart. Put your finger on the heart. Look at the picture of** *toast* **by the heart. The ending sound in** *toast* **is /st/. What are the letters for the sound /st/? Circle the letters for the sound /st/.**

Scoring: For each child, mark the answer to each question correct or incorrect. Then count the total number correct for each child. Using the guidelines below, record the child's score on the Individual Record for the Unit 4 Benchmark Assessment (T57).

Number Correct	Rating	
8	Proficient	+
6 – 7	Developing	✓
Less than 6	Emerging	–

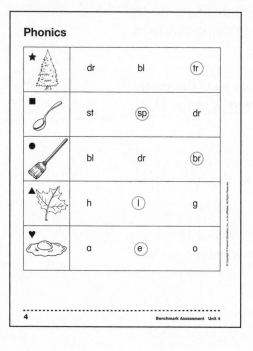

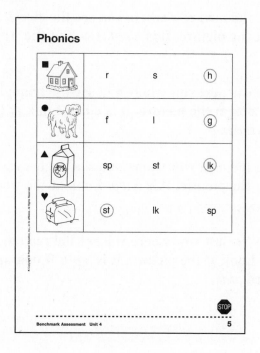

3. Word Reading

(Individual or small group)

Purpose: Assesses ability to read CVC words.

Hand out student page 6. Use the following directions to administer the assessment, beginning with the sample question.

Now we are going to find some words you know. Let's do the first one together. Find the small star. Put your finger on it. Now look at the picture by the star. It is a _cat._ Look at the three words in the same row. Which word spells _cat?_ (Pause.) **Yes, the first word in the row is _cat. Cat_ is spelled _c, a, t._ Draw a circle around the word _cat._**

When you are sure that each child understands the task and has followed the directions for completing the sample item, administer each test item.

1. **Move down to the next row where you see the square. Put your finger on the square. Look at the picture. It is a _bed._ Look at the words in the row. Circle the word _bed._**

2. **Move down to the next row where you see the circle. Put your finger on the circle. Look at the picture. It is a _hat._ Look at the words in the row. Circle the word _hat._**

3. **Move down to the next row where you see the triangle. Put your finger on the triangle. Look at the picture. It is a _net._ Look at the words in the row. Circle the word _net._**

4. **Move down to the next row where you see the heart. Put your finger on the heart. Look at the picture. It is a _top._ Look at the words in the row. Circle the word _top._**

5. **Move down to the last row where you see the rectangle. Put your finger on the rectangle. Look at the picture. It is a _pin._ Look at the words in the row. Circle the word _pin._**

Scoring: For each child, mark the answer to each question correct or incorrect. Then count the total number correct for each child. Using the guidelines below, record the child's score on the Individual Record for the Unit 4 Benchmark Assessment (T57).

Number Correct	Rating	
5	Proficient	+
3 – 4	Developing	✓
Less than 3	Emerging	–

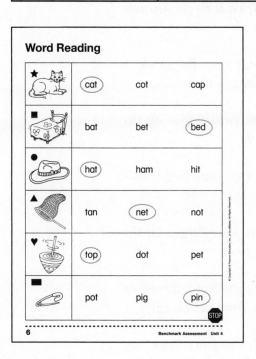

4. Word Knowledge: High-Frequency Words
(Individual or small group)

Purpose: Assesses ability to recognize high-frequency words.

Hand out student pages 7–8. Move through the assessment quickly to be sure you are assessing the child's ability to recognize the high-frequency words quickly.

1. **Let's find some words you know. I am going to say a word and ask you to draw a circle around that word. Find the star in the top row. Put your finger on it. Now look at the three words in that row. Draw a circle around the word *are . . . are.***

2. **Move down to the next row where you see the square. Put your finger on the square. Look at the three words. Circle the word *that . . . that.***

3. **Move down to the next row where you see the circle. Put your finger on the circle. Look at the three words. Circle the word *do . . . do.***

4. **Move down to the next row where you see the triangle. Put your finger on the triangle. Look at the three words. Circle the word *one . . . one.***

5. **Move down to the next row where you see the heart. Put your finger on the heart. Look at the three words. Circle the word *two . . . two.***

6. **Move down to the next row where you see the rectangle. Put your finger on the rectangle. Look at the three words. Circle the word *three . . . three.***

7. **Move down to the next row where you see the diamond. Put your finger on the diamond. Look at the three words. Circle the word *four . . . four.***

8. **Move down to the next row where you see the oval. Put your finger on the oval. Look at the three words. Circle the word *five . . . five.***

9. **Now go to the top of the next page. Look at the top row where you see the square. Put your finger on the square. Look at the three words. Circle the word *here . . . here.***

10. **Move down to the next row where you see the circle. Put your finger on the circle. Look at the three words. Circle the word *go . . . go.***

11. **Move down to the last row where you see the triangle. Put your finger on the triangle. Look at the three words. Circle the word *from . . . from.***

- - - - - - - - **Word Knowledge: High-Frequency Words** -

Scoring: For each child, count the total number of words circled correctly. Using the guidelines below, record the child's score on the Individual Record for the Unit 4 Benchmark Assessment (T57).

Number Correct	Rating	
11	Proficient	+
8 – 10	Developing	✓
Less than 8	Emerging	–

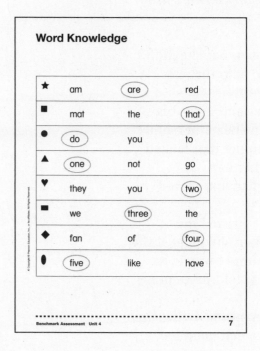

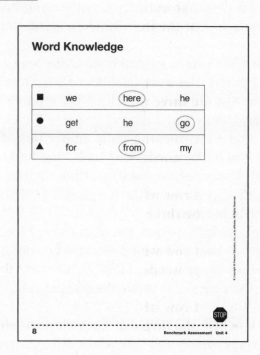

5. Listening Comprehension: Sequence

(Individual, small group, or whole class)

Purpose: Assesses general comprehension.

Hand out student page 9. Read aloud the introduction and the story printed in **bold.** Then read each question that follows. Children are to respond by circling the best answer to each question.

I am going to read a story about Ricky's mother and her hobby. Then I will ask you some questions. Listen carefully. Here is the story.

Ricky's mother had a very special hobby. She was a clown, but she didn't work in a circus. Instead, she went to children's hospitals to help the sick children feel better. She did that by making them laugh.

Every Saturday, Ricky's mother put on great big clothes and great big clown shoes. She painted a great big smile on her face. Then she gathered her bag of tricks. She had balloons. She had balls. She had a puppet that looked like a white rabbit. Ricky helped out by putting the bag in her car.

Then Ricky's mother drove to the hospital. People laughed and waved when they saw her in her car.

At the hospital, Ricky's mother put on a show. First she twisted the balloons into funny animals. She gave one to every child. Then she juggled the balls. She hardly ever dropped one. Finally, she made the puppet wiggle its rabbit nose and rabbit ears. She made the puppet talk too. It told jokes in a funny voice.

The children laughed and laughed. They clapped and clapped. By the time the show was over, they really did feel better. Ricky's mother felt good too.

Now I am going to ask you some questions about the story. For each question there are three pictures. Draw a circle around the picture that shows the best answer. Listen carefully.

1. **Look at the first row of pictures at the top of the page where you see the square. Put your finger on the square. What did Ricky's mother do first in the story? Circle the picture that shows what Ricky's mother did first.**

2. **Move down to the next row of pictures where you see the circle. Put your finger on the circle. What kind of clown face did Ricky's mother paint on—sad, happy, or angry? Circle the picture that shows what kind of clown face she painted on.**

3. **Move down to the next row of pictures where you see the heart. Put your finger on the heart. What did Ricky do to help his mother? Circle the picture that shows how Ricky helped his mother.**

4. **Move down to the next row of pictures where you see the triangle. Put your finger on the triangle. What did people do when they saw Ricky's mother in her car? Circle the picture that shows what people did when they saw Ricky's mother in her car.**

5. **Move down to the last row of pictures where you see the rectangle. Put your finger on the rectangle. What happened last in the story? Circle the picture that shows what happened last in the story.**

Scoring: For each child, mark the answer to each question correct or incorrect. Then count the total number correct for each child. Using the guidelines below, record the child's score on the Individual Record for the Unit 4 Benchmark Assessment (T57).

Number Correct	Rating	
5	Proficient	+
3 – 4	Developing	✓
Less than 3	Emerging	–

6. Writing: Sentences

(Individual, small group, or whole class)

Purpose: Assesses ability to write a sentence.

Hand out student page 10. Instruct children as follows.

Remember that a sentence tells something. Draw a picture. Then write a sentence that tells something about your picture.

Scoring: Using the guidelines below, evaluate the child's work and record the child's score on the Individual Record for the Unit 4 Benchmark Assessment (T57).

Scoring Guidelines	Rating	
The child draws a recognizable picture and writes a sentence that tells about the picture.	Proficient	+
The child draws a reasonable picture and writes some words or can dictate a sentence.	Developing	✓
The child draws a picture and attempts to write or dictate a sentence, but both are less than complete and correct.	Emerging	–

Writing

STOP

10   Benchmark Assessment   Unit 4

- - - **Writing: Sentences** -

INDIVIDUAL RECORD

Unit 4 Benchmark Assessment

Child's Name _____ **Date** _____

Directions: Record the results of the Unit 4 Benchmark Assessment by marking Proficient (+), Developing (✓), or Emerging (–) beside each assessed skill.

Unit 4 Assessed Skills	Proficient (+)	Developing (✓)	Emerging (–)	Common Core State Standard
Phonemic Awareness: Recognizing Initial and Final Sounds				Foundational Skills 2.d.
Phonics: Letter-Sound Correspondence (*h, l, g,* short *e, st-, sp-, tr-, bl-, br-, dr-, -st, -sp, -lk*)				Foundational Skills 3.a., 3.b.
Word Reading: CVC Words				Foundational Skills 3.
Word Knowledge: High-Frequency Words				Foundational Skills 3.c.
Listening Comprehension: Sequence				Literature 3.
Writing: Sentences				Writing 2.

Notes/Observations

UNIT 5 DIRECTIONS

1. Phonemic Awareness: Recognizing Initial (/w/, /j/, short *u*, /v/, /z/, /y/, /kw/) and Final Sounds (/z/, /ks/)
(Individual or small group)

Purpose: Assesses ability to recognize initial sounds and final sounds.

Hand out student pages 2–3. Use the following directions to administer the test, beginning with the sample question. Directions in **bold** are to be read aloud. The others are for your information only.

We are going to listen for sounds in words. Find the small star. Put your finger on it. Now look at the three pictures in the row beside the star: *jacks, whale, jam.* **Listen to the beginning sound of each word:** *jacks, whale, jam.* **Two of the words begin with the same sound. One of the words begins with a different sound. Which two words have the same beginning sound?** (Pause.) **Yes,** *jacks* **and** *jam* **have the same beginning sound. Draw a circle around the pictures of the** *jacks* **and the** *jam.*

When you are sure that each child understands the task and has followed the directions for completing the sample item, administer each test item.

1. **Move down to the next row where you see the square. Put your finger on the square. Now look at the three pictures in the same row:** *web, wing, horse.* **Circle the two pictures that have the same sound at the beginning:** *web . . . wing . . . horse.*

2. **Move down to the next row where you see the circle. Put your finger on the circle. Look at the three pictures in that row:** *violin, nail, van.* **Circle the two pictures that have the same sound at the beginning:** *violin . . . nail . . . van.*

3. **Move down to the next row where you see the triangle. Put your finger on the triangle. Look at the three pictures in that row:** *jar, jet, goat.* **Circle the two pictures that have the same sound at the beginning:** *jar . . . jet . . . goat.*

4. **Move down to the next row where you see the heart. Put your finger on the heart. Look at the three pictures in that row:** *apple, umbrella, up.* **Circle the two pictures that have the same sound at the beginning:** *apple . . . umbrella . . . up.*

5. **Go to the top of the next page. Look at the top row where you see the square. Put your finger on the square. Look at the three pictures in that row:** *zebra, monkey, zipper.* **Circle the two pictures that have the same sound at the beginning:** *zebra . . . monkey . . . zipper.*

6. **Move down to the next row where you see the circle. Put your finger on the circle. Look at the three pictures in that row:** *watch, yo-yo, yarn.* **Circle the two pictures that have the same sound at the beginning:** *watch . . . yo-yo . . . yarn.*

7. **Move down to the next row where you see the triangle. Put your finger on the triangle. Look at the three pictures in that row:** *fence, queen, quilt.* **Circle the two pictures that have the same sound at the beginning:** *fence . . . queen . . . quilt.*

8. **Move down to the next row where you see the heart. Put your finger on the heart. Look at the three pictures in that row. Listen for the ending sound:** *rose, sock, sneeze.* **Circle the two pictures that have the same sound at the end:** *rose . . . sock . . . sneeze.*

9. **Move down to the last row where you see the rectangle. Put your finger on the rectangle. Look at the three pictures in that row. Listen for the ending sound:** *box, kite, six.* **Circle the two pictures that have the same sound at the end:** *box . . . kite . . . six.*

Scoring: For each child, mark the answer to each question correct or incorrect. Then count the total number correct for each child. Using the guidelines below, record the child's score on the Individual Record for the Unit 5 Benchmark Assessment (T70).

Number Correct	Rating	
9	Proficient	+
7 – 8	Developing	✓
Less than 7	Emerging	–

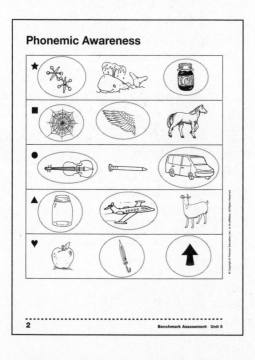

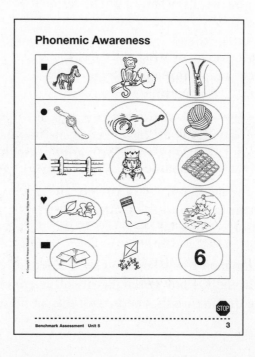

2. Phonics: Letter-Sound Correspondence (*w, j, v, y, qu,* short *u, -x, -z*)

(Individual or small group)

Purpose: Assesses ability to connect sound to letter.

Hand out student pages 4–5. Use the following directions to administer the assessment, beginning with the sample question.

Now we are going to match a letter to its sound. Let's do the first one together. Find the small star. Put your finger on it. Now look at the letter by the star. It is the letter *j*. What is the sound of the letter *j*? (Have a child give the sound of the letter *j*.) **Now look at the three pictures in the same row: *sun, jar, fish*. Which word begins with the sound of the letter *j*?** (Pause.) **Yes, *jar* begins with the sound of the letter *j*. Draw a circle around the picture of the *jar* because *jar* begins with the letter *j*.**

When you are sure that each child understands the task and has followed the directions for completing the sample item, administer each test item.

1. **Move down to the next row where you see the square. Put your finger on the square. Look at the *w*. Look at the pictures: *worm, bird, vest*. Circle the picture that begins with the sound of the letter *w*.**

2. **Move down to the next row where you see the circle. Put your finger on the circle. Look at the *u*. Look at the pictures: *egg, umbrella, igloo*. Circle the picture that begins with the sound of the letter *u*.**

3. **Move down to the next row where you see the triangle. Put your finger on the triangle. Look at the *v*. Look at the pictures: *van, whale, ten*. Circle the picture that begins with the sound of the letter *v*.**

4. **Move down to the next row where you see the heart. Put your finger on the heart. Look at the *y*. Look at the pictures: *yarn, pen, fence*. Circle the picture that begins with the sound of the letter *y*.**

5. **Go to the next page. Look at the top row where you see the square. Put your finger on the square. Look at the *qu*. Look at the pictures: *hen, queen, vase*. Circle the picture that begins with the sound of the letters *qu*.**

6. **Move down to the next row where you see the circle. Put your finger on the circle. Look at the *j*. Look at the pictures: *bus, train, jet*. Circle the picture that begins with the sound of the letter *j*.**

7. **Move down to the next row where you see the triangle. Put your finger on the triangle. Look at the *x*. Look at the pictures. Listen for the ending sound: *fox, mat, dog*. Circle the picture that ends with the sound of the letter *x*.**

8. Move down to the next row where you see the heart. Put your finger on the heart. Look at the z. Look at the pictures. Listen for the ending sound: *goat, hand, maze*. Circle the picture that ends with the sound of the letter *z*.

Scoring: For each child, mark the answer to each question correct or incorrect. Then count the total number correct for each child. Using the guidelines below, record the child's score on the Individual Record for the Unit 5 Benchmark Assessment (T70).

Number Correct	Rating	
8	Proficient	+
6 – 7	Developing	✓
Less than 6	Emerging	–

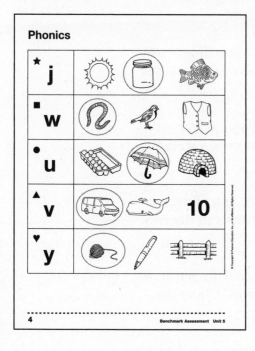

3. Word Reading
(Individual or small group)

Purpose: Assesses ability to read CVC words.

Hand out student pages 6–7. Use the following directions to administer the assessment, beginning with the sample question.

Now we are going to circle some words you know. Let's do the first one together. Find the small star. Put your finger on it. Now look at the picture by the star. It is a *cup*. Now look at the three words in the same row. Which word spells *cup*? (Pause.) **Yes, the last word in the row is *cup*. *Cup* is spelled c, u, p . . . cup. Draw a circle around the word *cup*.**

When you are sure that each child understands the task and has followed the directions for completing the sample item, administer each test item.

1. **Move down to the next row where you see the square. Put your finger on it. Look at the picture. It is a *pin*. Look at the words in the row. Circle the word *pin*.**

2. **Move down to the next row where you see the circle. Put your finger on it. Look at the picture. It is a *bat*. Look at the words in the row. Circle the word *bat*.**

3. **Move down to the next row where you see the triangle. Put your finger on it. Look at the picture. It is the number *ten*. Look at the words in the row. Circle the word *ten*.**

4. **Move down to the next row where you see the heart. Put your finger on it. Look at the picture. It is a *box*. Look at the words in the row. Circle the word *box*.**

5. **Go to the next page. Look at the top row where you see the square. Put your finger on it. Look at the picture. It is a *log*. Look at the words in the row. Circle the word *log*.**

6. **Move down to the next row where you see the circle. Put your finger on it. Look at the picture. It is a *man*. Look at the words in the row. Circle the word *man*.**

7. **Move down to the next row where you see the triangle. Put your finger on it. Look at the picture. It is a *sun*. Look at the words in the row. Circle the word *sun*.**

8. **Move down to the last row where you see the heart. Put your finger on it. Look at the picture. It is a *bib*. Look at the words in the row. Circle the word *bib*.**

Scoring: For each child, mark the answer to each question correct or incorrect. Then count the total number correct for each child. Using the guidelines below, record the child's score on the Individual Record for the Unit 5 Benchmark Assessment (T70).

Number Correct	Rating	
8	Proficient	+
6 – 7	Developing	✓
Less than 6	Emerging	–

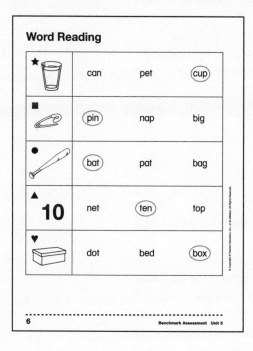

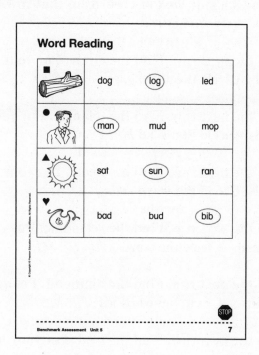

4. Word Knowledge: High-Frequency Words

(Individual or small group)

Purpose: Assesses ability to recognize high-frequency words.

Hand out student page 8. Children are to circle each word as you say it aloud. Move through the assessment quickly to be sure you are assessing the child's ability to recognize the high-frequency words quickly.

1. **Now we are going to circle some words you know. Find the square. Put your finger on it. Now look at the three words in that row. Draw a circle around the word** *yellow . . . yellow.*

2. **Move down to the next row. Find the circle. Put your finger on it. Look at the three words. Circle the word** *green . . . green.*

3. **Move down to the next row. Find the triangle. Put your finger on it. Look at the three words. Circle the word** *blue . . . blue.*

4. **Move down to the next row. Find the heart. Put your finger on it. Look at the three words. Circle the word** *what . . . what.*

5. **Move down to the next row. Find the rectangle. Put your finger on it. Look at the three words. Circle the word** *said . . . said.*

6. **Move down to the next row. Find the diamond. Put your finger on it. Look at the three words. Circle the word** *was . . . was.*

7. **Move down to the next row. Find the oval. Put your finger on it. Look at the three words. Circle the word** *where . . . where.*

8. **Move down to the last row. Find the stop-sign shape. Put your finger on it. Look at the three words. Circle the word** *come . . . come.*

Scoring: For each child, count the total number of words circled correctly. Using the guidelines below, record the child's score on the Individual Record for the Unit 5 Benchmark Assessment (T70).

Number Correct	Rating	
8	Proficient	+
6 – 7	Developing	✓
Less than 6	Emerging	–

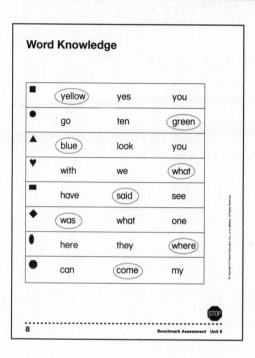

5. Listening Comprehension: Plot

(Individual, small group, or whole class)

Purpose: Assesses general comprehension.

Hand out student page 9. Read aloud the introduction and the story printed in **bold**. Then read each question that follows. Children are to respond by circling the best answer to each question.

I am going to read a story about a king and his cook. Then I will ask you some questions. Listen carefully. Here is the story.

Once upon a time there was a king named Frederick who lived in a tall castle high on a bright green hill. King Frederick had a fine white horse to ride, a bright golden crown to wear, a lot of money, and a cook to bring him tasty meals.

But King Frederick was not happy.

"I am so bored it makes me angry!" he told the castle cook one day. "I do not like being king anymore."

The cook's name was Martin. "What would you like to be instead?" Martin the cook asked.

King Frederick looked down at the tasty meal that Martin had set before him. The meat and vegetables smelled so delicious.

"I know," said King Frederick to Martin the cook. "I would like to do what you do. Let's trade places, Martin. What do you say?"

"Oh yes," Martin said, for he had always dreamed of being king.

So Frederick gave Martin his crown and went skipping happily off to the kitchen. Now he, Frederick, was the castle cook. Meanwhile, Martin put on the heavy crown and sat on the golden throne. Now he, Martin, was king. "Hooray for King Martin!" Martin shouted.

But King Martin soon grew lonesome, sitting on the throne under that heavy crown all day long. Martin missed his meats and vegetables and pots and pans. He wanted to be Martin the cook again. Meanwhile, Frederick was growing lonesome too. Cooking was hard work. He missed his fine white horse and golden crown. He wanted to be Frederick the king again.

So the next day, the two men agreed to trade places again and go back to being their old selves. Frederick became King Frederick again, wearing his golden crown, and Martin became the castle cook again, making the king's meals like always, with a big, happy smile on his face.

Now I am going to ask you some questions about the story. For each question there are three pictures. Draw a circle around the picture that shows the best answer. Listen carefully.

1. Look at the first row of pictures where you see the square. Put your finger on the square. Who is this story about? Circle the picture that shows who this story is about.

2. Move down to the next row of pictures where you see the circle. Put your finger on the circle. How did King Frederick feel at the beginning of the story—happy, angry, or silly? Circle the picture that shows how King Frederick felt at the beginning of the story.

3. Move down to the next row of pictures where you see the triangle. Put your finger on the triangle. What did King Frederick give to Martin, his cook? Circle the picture that shows what King Frederick gave to his cook.

4. Move down to the next row of pictures where you see the heart. Put your finger on the heart. After trading places with King Frederick, what did Martin do all day long? Circle the picture that shows what Martin did all day long after trading places with the king.

5. Move down to the last row of pictures where you see the rectangle. Put your finger on the rectangle. How did Martin feel at the end of the story—happy, tired, or scared? Circle the picture that shows how Martin felt at the end of the story.

Scoring: For each child, mark the answer to each question correct or incorrect. Then count the total number correct for each child. Using the guidelines below, record the child's score on the Individual Record for the Unit 5 Benchmark Assessment (T70).

Number Correct	Rating	
5	Proficient	+
3 – 4	Developing	✓
Less than 3	Emerging	−

6. Writing: Questions

(Individual, small group, or whole class)

Purpose: Assesses ability to write a question.

Hand out student page 10. Instruct children as follows.

Remember that a question asks something. Draw a picture. Then write a question that asks something about your picture.

Scoring: Using the guidelines below, evaluate the child's work and record the child's score on the Individual Record for the Unit 5 Benchmark Assessment (T70).

Scoring Guidelines	Rating	
The child draws a recognizable picture and writes a question that is appropriate and generally written correctly.	Proficient	+
The child draws a reasonable picture and writes a question or part of a question about the picture, but words may include a few errors.	Developing	✓
The child draws a picture and attempts to write a question, but both are less than complete and correct.	Emerging	–

- -

INDIVIDUAL RECORD

Unit 5 Benchmark Assessment

Child's Name _____ **Date** _____

Directions: Record the results of the Unit 5 Benchmark Assessment by marking
Proficient (+), Developing (✓), or Emerging (–) beside each assessed skill.

Unit 5 Assessed Skills	Proficient (+)	Developing (✓)	Emerging (–)	Common Core State Standard
Phonemic Awareness: Recognizing Initial Sounds and Final Sounds (/w/, /j/, short *u*, /v/, /z/, /y/, /kw/, /ks/, /z/)				Foundational Skills 2.d.
Phonics: Letter-Sound Correspondence: (*w, j, v, y, qu,* short *u, -x, -z*)				Foundational Skills 3.a., 3.b.
Word Reading: CVC Words				Foundational Skills 3.
Word Knowledge: High-Frequency Words				Foundational Skills 3.c.
Listening Comprehension: Plot				Literature 3.
Writing: Questions				Writing 2.

Notes/Observations

UNIT 6 DIRECTIONS

1. Phonemic Awareness: Blending Individual Phonemes
(Individual or small group)

Purpose: Assesses ability to blend individual phonemes.

Hand out student pages 2–3. Use the following directions to administer the test, beginning with the sample question.

Directions in **bold** are to be read aloud; others are for your information only.

We are going to listen to sounds in a word. Find the small star. Put your finger on it. Now look at the three pictures in that row. I am going to say a word. Listen to the sounds I say: /k/ /a/ /p/. Blend the sounds together. What word is it? (Pause.) **Yes, the word is** *cap.* **Which picture goes with the word /k/ /a/ /p/? Yes, the middle picture is a /k/ /a/ /p/ . . .** *cap.* **Draw a circle around the picture of the cap in the middle.**

When you are sure that each child understands the task and has followed the directions for completing the sample item, administer each test item.

1. **Move down to the next row where you see the square. Put your finger on it. Look at the three pictures in that row. Which picture is a /f/ /o/ /ks/? Circle the picture of the /f/ /o/ /ks/.**

2. **Move down to the next row where you see the circle. Put your finger on it. Look at the three pictures in that row. Which picture is a /h/ /i/ /l/? Circle the picture of the /h/ /i/ /l/.**

3. **Move down to the next row where you see the triangle. Put your finger on it. Look at the three pictures in that row. Which picture is a /b/ /a/ /g/? Circle the picture of the /b/ /a/ /g/.**

4. **Move down to the next row where you see the heart. Put your finger on it. Look at the three pictures in that row. Which picture is a /n/ /e/ /s/ /t/? Circle the picture of the /n/ /e/ /s/ /t/.**

5. **Go to the next page. Look at the top row where you see the square. Put your finger on it. Look at the three pictures in that row. Which picture is a /p/ /e/ /n/? Circle the picture of the /p/ /e/ /n/.**

6. **Move down to the next row where you see the circle. Put your finger on it. Look at the three pictures in that row. Which picture is a /w/ /e/ /b/? Circle the picture of the /w/ /e/ /b/.**

7. **Move down to the next row where you see the triangle. Put your finger on it. Look at the three pictures in that row. Which picture is a /t/ /r/ /u/ /k/? Circle the picture of the /t/ /r/ /u/ /k/.**

8. Move down to the last row where you see the heart. Put your finger on it. Look at the three pictures in that row. Which picture is a /v/ /e/ /s/ /t/? Circle the picture of the /v/ /e/ /s/ /t/.

Scoring: For each child, mark the answer to each question correct or incorrect. Then count the total number correct for each child. Using the guidelines below, record the child's score on the Individual Record for the Unit 6 Benchmark Assessment (T80).

Number Correct	Rating	
8	Proficient	+
6 – 7	Developing	✓
Less than 6	Emerging	–

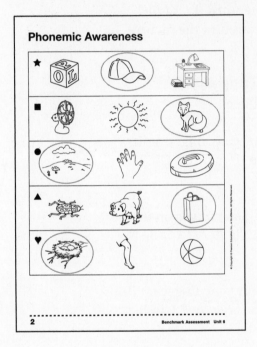

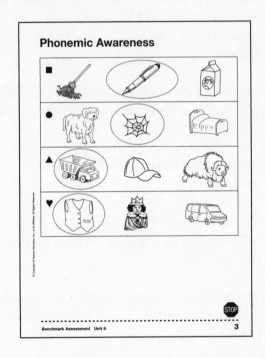

2. Word Reading
(Individual or small group)

Purpose: Assesses ability to read CVC and CCVC words.

Hand out student pages 4–5. Use the following directions to administer the assessment, beginning with the sample question.

Now we are going to circle words. Let's do the first one together. Find the small star. Put your finger on it. Now look at the picture by the star. It is a *pen*. Look at the three words in the same row. Which word is *pen*? (Pause.) **Yes, the middle word in the row is *pen: p, e, n . . . pen*. Draw a circle around the word *pen*.**

When you are sure that each child understands the task and has followed the directions for completing the sample item, administer each test item.

1. **Move down to the next row where you see the square. Put your finger on it. Look at the picture. It is a *step*. Look at the three words in the row. Circle the word *step . . . step*.**

2. **Move down to the next row where you see the circle. Put your finger on it. Look at the picture. It is a *bug*. Look at the three words in the row. Circle the word *bug . . . bug*.**

3. **Move down to the next row where you see the triangle. Put your finger on it. Look at the picture. The arrow is pointing to a fish's *fin*. Look at the three words in the row. Circle the word *fin . . . fin*.**

4. **Move down to the next row where you see the heart. Put your finger on it. Look at the picture. It is a *box*. Look at the three words in the row. Circle the word *box . . . box*.**

5. **Go to the next page. Look at the top row where you see the square. Put your finger on it. Look at the picture. It is a *jet*. Look at the three words in the row. Circle the word *jet . . . jet*.**

6. **Move down to the next row where you see the circle. Put your finger on it. Look at the picture. It is a *map*. Look at the three words in the row. Circle the word *map . . . map*.**

7. **Move down to the next row where you see the triangle. Put your finger on it. Look at the picture. It is a *tub*. Look at the three words in the row. Circle the word *tub . . . tub*.**

8. **Move down to the last row where you see the heart. Put your finger on it. Look at the picture. It is a *van*. Look at the three words in the row. Circle the word *van . . . van*.**

Scoring: For each child, mark the answer to each question correct or incorrect. Then count the total number correct for each child. Using the guidelines below, record the child's score on the Individual Record for the Unit 6 Benchmark Assessment (T80).

Number Correct	Rating	
8	Proficient	+
6 – 7	Developing	✓
Less than 6	Emerging	–

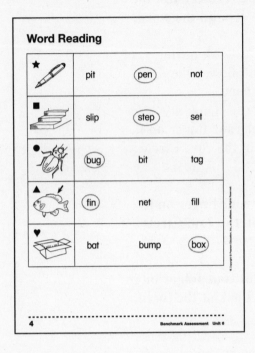

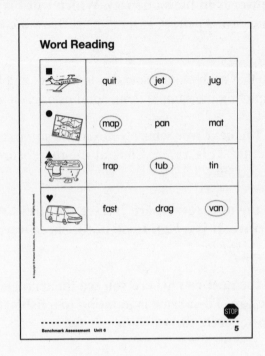

3. Word Knowledge: High-Frequency Words
(Individual or small group)

Purpose: Assesses ability to immediately recognize high-frequency words.

Hand out student pages 6–7. Children are to circle each word as you say it aloud. Move through the assessment quickly to make sure you are assessing the child's ability to recognize the high-frequency words quickly.

1. I am going to say one word in each row. You are going to circle the word I say. Find the first row with the square in it. Put your finger on it. Now look at the three words in that row. Draw a circle around the word *go . . . go*.

2. Move down to the next row. Put your finger on the circle. Look at the three words. Circle the word *said . . . said*.

3. Move down to the next row. Put your finger on the triangle. Look at the three words. Circle the word *come . . . come*.

4. Move down to the next row. Put your finger on the heart. Look at the three words. Circle the word *are . . . are*.

5. Move down to the next row. Put your finger on the rectangle. Look at the three words. Circle the word *two . . . two*.

6. Move down to the next row. Put your finger on the diamond. Look at the three words. Circle the word *five . . . five*.

7. Move down to the next row. Put your finger on the oval. Look at the three words. Circle the word *do . . . do*.

8. Go to the next page. Look at the top row with the square in it. Put your finger on the square. Look at the three words. Circle the word *green . . . green*.

9. Move down to the next row. Put your finger on the circle. Look at the three words. Circle the word *what . . . what*.

10. Move down to the last row. Put your finger on the triangle. Look at the three words. Circle the word *one . . . one*.

Scoring: For each child, count the total number of words circled correctly. Using the guidelines below, record the child's score on the Individual Record for the Unit 6 Benchmark Assessment (T80).

Number Correct	Rating	
10	Proficient	+
8 – 9	Developing	✓
Less than 8	Emerging	–

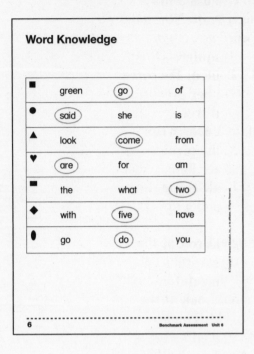

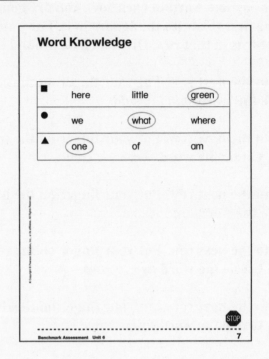

4. Listening Comprehension: Character, Setting, Plot
(Individual, small group, or whole class)

Purpose: Assesses general comprehension.

Hand out student page 8. Read aloud the introduction and the story printed in **bold.** Then read each question that follows. Children are to respond by circling the best answer to each question.

I am going to read a story about a cat named Maggie. Then I will ask you some questions. Listen carefully. Here is the story.

Maggie was an old cat who lived in a garden with birds and squirrels and snakes. She had a little house in the back of the yard. When it rained, Maggie would go into her little house in a corner of the garden and sit on her green pillow. From there she could watch the rain fall on the bushes and trees.

The family Maggie belonged to gave her two meals every day. One was breakfast, and the other was dinner. They put Maggie's bowl on the picnic table in the garden. In the morning, Maggie would eat only half her food. She would save the other half so that she could have snacks during the day. At dinnertime, she did the same thing. She would eat only half her food and save the rest to snack on at night.

The squirrels who lived in the garden enjoyed Maggie's snacks too. A squirrel would run to Maggie's bowl, take one piece of food, and scramble up a tree. Maggie did not mind sharing with the squirrels because they did not eat many snacks.

Then one day some sparrows began to snack on Maggie's food. The birds flew down from the tree and perched on Maggie's bowl. They pecked away at the food that was left in the bowl. Soon all Maggie's food was gone. This happened the next day, too.

Maggie had a problem, but she knew what she had to do about it. She began to eat her breakfast slowly until she finished it all. She did the same thing with her dinner. She didn't leave any food for the sparrows to steal. She didn't have any food left for snacks, but she never felt hungry because she was very full from eating all her food at one time. The sparrows in the garden found out that an old cat can learn new tricks.

Now I am going to ask you some questions about the story. For each question there are three pictures. Draw a circle around the picture that shows the best answer. Listen carefully.

1. **Look at the first row of pictures at the top of the page where you see the square. Put your finger on the square. What kind of animal was Maggie? Circle the picture that shows what kind of animal Maggie is.**

2. **Move down to the next row of pictures where you see the circle. Put your finger on the circle. Where did Maggie live? Circle the picture that shows where Maggie lived.**

3. **Move down to the next row of pictures where you see the triangle. Put your finger on the triangle. Where did Maggie go when it rained? Circle the picture that shows where Maggie went when it rained.**

4. **Move down to the next row of pictures where you see the heart. Put your finger on the heart. What animals ate all of Maggie's food? Circle the picture that shows what animals ate all of Maggie's food.**

5. **Move down to the last row of pictures where you see the rectangle. Put your finger on the rectangle. What did Maggie's food bowl look like at the end of the story? Circle the picture that shows what Maggie's food bowl looked like at the end of the story.**

Scoring: For each child, mark the answer to each question correct or incorrect. Then count the total number correct for each child. Using the guidelines below, record the child's score on the Individual Record for the Unit 6 Benchmark Assessment (T80).

Number Correct	Rating	
5	Proficient	+
3 – 4	Developing	✓
Less than 3	Emerging	–

5. Writing: Sentences or Questions
(Individual, small group, or whole class)

Purpose: Assesses ability to write a sentence or a question.

Hand out student page 9. Instruct children as follows.

Remember that a sentence tells something. Remember that a question asks something. Draw a picture. Then write a sentence or a question about it.

Note: If children have trouble thinking of something to draw, remind them of what they have learned in the selections about things that people and animals build.

Scoring: Using the guidelines below, evaluate the child's work and record the child's score on the Individual Record for the Unit 6 Benchmark Assessment (T80).

Scoring Guidelines	Rating	
The child draws a recognizable picture and writes a sentence or question that is appropriate and generally written correctly.	Proficient	+
The child draws a reasonable picture and writes a sentence, or question, or part of a sentence or question about the picture, but words may include a few errors.	Developing	✓
The child draws a picture and attempts to write a sentence or question, but both are less than complete and correct.	Emerging	−

Writing

STOP

Benchmark Assessment Unit 6   9

INDIVIDUAL RECORD

Unit 6 Benchmark Assessment

Child's Name _____ Date _____

Directions: Record the results of the Unit 6 Benchmark Assessment by marking
Proficient (+), Developing (✓), or Emerging (–) beside each assessed skill.

Unit 6 Assessed Skills	Proficient (+)	Developing (✓)	Emerging (–)	Common Core State Standard
Phonemic Awareness: Blending Individual Phonemes				Foundational Skills 2.c.
Word Reading: CVC and CCVC Words				Foundational Skills 3.
Word Knowledge: High-Frequency Words				Foundational Skills 3.c.
Listening Comprehension: Character, Setting, Plot				Literature 3.
Writing: Sentences or Questions				Writing 2.

Notes/Observations

END-OF-YEAR ASSESSMENT DIRECTIONS

1. Phonemic Awareness: Recognizing Initial and Final Sounds and Blending Individual Phonemes

(Individual or small group)

Purpose: Assesses ability to recognize initial sounds and final sounds and to blend individual phonemes.

Hand out student pages 2–4. Use the first set of directions to administer the first nine questions of the test, beginning with the sample question. Then, read the second set of directions and the sample question before questions 10–13. Directions in **bold** are to be read aloud. Others are for your information only.

We are going to listen for sounds in words. Find the small star. Put your finger on it. Now look at the three pictures in the row beside the star: *lamb . . . mask . . . ladder.* **Listen to the beginning sound of each word:** *lamb, mask, ladder.* **Two of the words begin with the same sound. One of the words begins with a different sound. Which two words have the same beginning sound?** (Pause). **Yes,** *lamb* **and** *ladder* **have the same beginning sound. Draw a circle around the pictures of the** *lamb* **and the** *ladder.*

When you are sure that each child understands the task and has followed the directions for completing the sample item, administer each test item.

1. **Move down to the next row where you see the square. Put your finger on the square. Now look at the three pictures in the same row:** *pencil, parrot, basket.* **Draw a circle around the two pictures that have the same sound at the beginning:** *pencil . . . parrot . . . basket.*

2. **Move down to the next row where you see the circle. Put your finger on the circle. Now look at the three pictures in the same row:** *gorilla, mouse, gas.* **Draw a circle around the two pictures that have the same sound at the beginning:** *gorilla . . . mouse . . . gas.*

3. **Move down to the next row where you see the triangle. Put your finger on the triangle. Now look at the three pictures in the same row:** *pumpkin, zebra, zipper.* **Draw a circle around the two pictures that have the same sound at the beginning:** *pumpkin . . . zebra . . . zipper.*

4. **Move down to the next row where you see the heart. Put your finger on the heart. Now look at the three pictures in the same row:** *octopus, ox, kangaroo.* **Draw a circle around the two pictures that have the same sound at the beginning:** *octopus . . . ox . . . kangaroo.*

5. **Go to the top of the next page. Look at the top row where you see the star. Put your finger on the star. Listen for the ending sound:** *cat, ball, hill.* **Draw a circle around the two pictures that have the same sound at the end:** *cat . . . ball . . . hill.*

6. Move down to the next row where you see the square. Put your finger on the square. Look at the pictures. Listen for the ending sound: *pen, coin, dog*. Draw a circle around the two pictures that have the same sound at the end: *pen . . . coin . . . dog.*

7. Move down to the next row where you see the circle. Put your finger on the circle. Look at the three pictures. Listen for the ending sound: *duck, bell, rock*. Draw a circle around the two pictures that have the same sound at the end: *duck . . . bell . . . rock.*

8. Move down to the next row where you see the triangle. Put your finger on the triangle. Look at the three pictures. Listen for the ending sound: *jar, fox, ax*. Draw a circle around the two pictures that have the same sound at the end: *jar . . . fox . . . ax.*

9. Move down to the next row where you see the heart. Put your finger on the heart. Look at the three pictures. Listen for the ending sound: walk, milk, nest. Draw a circle around the two pictures that have the same sound at the end: *walk . . . milk . . . nest.*

Go to the top of the next page. Now we are going to do something a little bit different. We are going to listen to all of the sounds in a word. Look at the top row where you see the star. Put your finger on the star. Now look at the three pictures in that row. I am going to say a word. Listen to the sounds I say: /m/ /a/ /p/. Blend the sounds together. What word is it? (Pause) Yes, the word is map. Which picture goes with the word /m/ /a/ /p/? Yes, the last picture is a /m/ /a/ /p/ . . . *map*. Draw a circle around the last picture of the map.

When you are sure that each child understands the task and has followed the directions for completing the sample item, administer each test item.

10. Move down to the next row where you see the square. Put your finger on it. Look at the three pictures in that row. Which picture is a /b/ /e/ /d/? Circle the picture of the /b/ /e/ /d/.

11. Move down to the next row where you see the circle. Put your finger on it. Look at the three pictures in that row. Which picture is a /w/ /i/ /g/? Circle the picture of the /w/ /i/ /g/.

12. Move down to the next row where you see the triangle. Put your finger on it. Look at the three pictures in that row. Which picture is a /s/ /o/ /k/? Circle the picture of the /s/ /o/ /k/.

13. Move down to the next row where you see the heart. Put your finger on it. Look at the three pictures in that row. Which picture is a /b/ /u/ /s/? Circle the picture of the /b/ /u/ /s/.

Scoring: For each child, mark the answer to each question correct or incorrect. Then count the total number correct for each child. Using the guidelines below, record the child's score in the Individual Record for the End-of-Year Assessment with alignments to Common Core State Standards (T96).

Number Correct	Rating	
12 – 13	Proficient	+
9 – 11	Developing	✓
Fewer than 9	Emerging	–

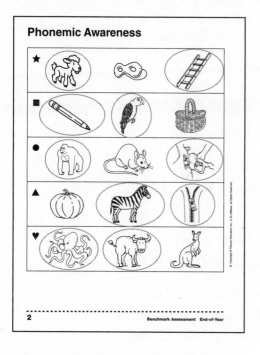

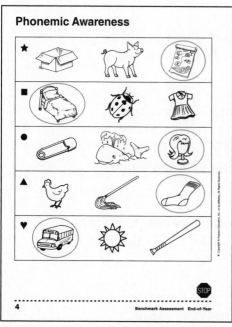

2. Phonics: Letter-Sound Correspondence

(Individual or small group)

Purpose: Assesses ability to connect sound to letter.

Hand out student pages 5–7. Use the following directions to administer the assessment, beginning with the sample question.

Now we are going to match a letter to its sound. Let's do the first one together. Find the small star. Put your finger on it. Now look at the letter by the star. It is the letter *r*. What is the sound of the letter *r*? (Have a child give the sound of the letter *r*.) **Now look at the three pictures in the same row: *ring* . . . *umbrella* . . . *van*. Which word begins with the sound of the letter *r*?** (Pause) **Yes, *ring* begins with the sound of the letter *r*. Draw a circle around the picture of the *ring* because *ring* begins with the letter *r*.**

When you are sure that each child understands the task and has followed the directions for completing the sample item, administer each test item.

1. **Move down to the next row where you see the square. Put your finger on the square. Look at the *d*. Look at the pictures: *dog* . . . *queen* . . . *tape*. Circle the picture that begins with the sound of the letter *d*.**

2. **Move down to the next row where you see the circle. Put your finger on the circle. Look at the *v*. Look at the pictures: *book* . . . *train* . . . *vine*. Circle the picture that begins with the sound of the letter *v*.**

3. **Move down to the next row where you see the triangle. Put your finger on the triangle. Look at the *f*. Look at the pictures: *bird* . . . *fan* . . . *car*. Circle the picture that begins with the sound of the letter *f*.**

4. **Move down to the next row where you see the heart. Put your finger on the heart. Look at the *n*. Look at the pictures: *nine* . . . *bee* . . . *clock*. Circle the picture that begins with the sound of the letter *n*.**

5. **Go to the next page. Now you will be listening for something different. You will be listening for the sound that ends a word. Look at the top row where you see the heart. Put your finger on the heart. Look at the *b*. Look at the pictures: *crab* . . . *door* . . . *wheel*. Circle the picture that ends with the sound of the letter *b*.**

6. **Move down to the next row where you see the circle. Put your finger on the circle. Look at the *g*. Look at the pictures: *tape* . . . *snail* . . . *dog*. Circle the picture that ends with the sound of the letter *g*.**

7. **Move down to the next row where you see the triangle. Put your finger on the triangle. Look at the *s*. Look at the pictures: *hand* . . . *dress* . . . *clown*. Circle the picture that ends with the sound of the letter *s*.**

8. Move down to the next row where you see the diamond. Put your finger on the diamond. Look at the *x*. Look at the pictures. Listen for the ending sound: *bat . . . box . . . nut*. Circle the picture that ends with the sound of the letter *x*.

9. Move down to the next row where you see the heart. Put your finger on the heart. Look at the *t*. Look at the pictures: *ax . . . foot . . . mouse*. Circle the picture that ends with the sound of the letter *t*.

Turn to the next page. Now we are going to find letters for a sound. Let's do the first one together. Find the small star. Put your finger on it. Now look at the picture by the star. It is a picture of a *block*. The beginning sound in *block* is /bl/. Now look at the letters in the same row. Which are letters for the sound /bl/? (Pause.) Yes, the first two letters in the row are the letters for the sound /bl/. Draw a circle around the letters *bl* because those are the letters for the sound /bl/.

10. Move down to the next row where you see the square. Put your finger on the square. Look at the picture of the *egg* by the square. The beginning sound in *egg* is /e/. What is the letter for the sound /e/? Circle the letter for the sound /e/.

11. Move down to the next row where you see the circle. Put your finger on the circle. Look at the picture of the *yarn* by the circle. The beginning sound in *yarn* is /y/. What is the letter for the sound /y/? Circle the letter for the sound /y/.

12. Move down to the next row where you see the triangle. Put your finger on the triangle. Look at the picture of the *drum* by the triangle. The beginning sound in *drum* is /dr/. What is the letter for the sound /dr/? Circle the letter for the sound /dr/.

13. Move down to the next row where you see the heart. Put your finger on the heart. Look at the picture of the *wasp* by the heart. The ending sound in *wasp* is /sp/. What is the letter for the sound /sp/? Circle the letter for the sound /sp/.

Scoring: For each child, mark the answer to each question correct or incorrect. Then count the total number correct for each child. Using the guidelines below, record the child's score in the Individual Record for the End-of-Year Assessment with alignments to Common Core State Standards (T96).

Number Correct	Rating	
13	Proficient	+
10 – 12	Developing	✓
Less than 10	Emerging	–

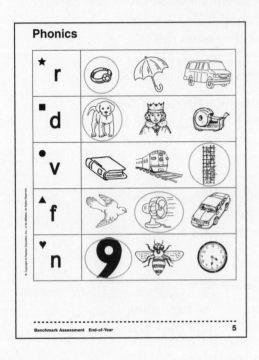

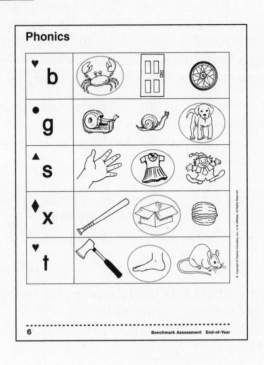

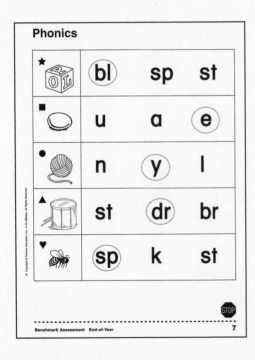

3. Word Reading

(Individual or small group)

Purpose: Assesses ability to read CVC, CVCC, and CCVC words.

Hand out student pages 8–10. Use the following directions to administer the assessment, beginning with the sample question.

Now we are going to circle words. Let's do the first one together. Find the small star. Put your finger on it. Now look at the picture by the star. It is a *fox*. Look at the three words in the same row. Which word is *fox*? (Pause.) **Yes, the middle word in the row is *fox: f, o, x . . . fox*. Draw a circle around the word *fox*.**

When you are sure that each child understands the task and has followed the directions for completing the sample item, administer each test item.

1. **Move down to the next row where you see the square. Put your finger on the square. Look at the picture. It shows *dig*. Look at the three words in the row. Circle the word *dig . . . dig*.**

2. **Move down to the next row where you see the circle. Put your finger on the circle. Look at the picture. It shows *gas*. Look at the three words in the row. Circle the word *gas . . . gas*.**

3. **Move down to the next row where you see the triangle. Put your finger on the triangle. Look at the picture. It is a *kiss*. Look at the three words in the row. Circle the word *kiss . . . kiss*.**

4. **Move down to the next row where you see the heart. Put your finger on the heart. Look at the picture. It is a *nut*. Look at the three words in the row. Circle the word *nut . . . nut*.**

5. **Go to the next page. Look at the top row where you see the star. Put your finger on the star. Look at the picture. It is a *rug*. Look at the three words in the row. Circle the word *rug . . . rug*.**

6. **Move down to the next row where you see the square. Put your finger on the square. Look at the picture. It is a *web*. Look at the three words in the row. Circle the word *web . . . web*.**

7. **Move down to the next row where you see the circle. Put your finger on the circle. Look at the picture. It shows a *hit*. Look at the three words in the row. Circle the word *hit . . . hit*.**

8. **Move down to the next row where you see the triangle. Put your finger on the triangle. Look at the picture. It shows a *drip*. Look at the three words in the row. Circle the word *drip . . . drip*.**

9. **Move down to the next row where you see the heart. Put your finger on the heart. Look at the picture. It is a** *spot.* **Look at the three words in the row. Circle the word** *spot . . . spot.*

10. **Go to the next page. Look at the top row where you see the square. Put your finger on the square. Look at the picture. It shows** *trip.* **Look at the three words in the row. Circle the word** *trip . . . trip.*

11. **Move down to the next row where you see the circle. Put your finger on the circle. Look at the picture. It is a** *vest.* **Look at the three words in the row. Circle the word** *vest . . . vest.*

12. **Move down to the next row where you see the triangle. Put your finger on the triangle. Look at the picture. It shows** *talk.* **Look at the three words in the row. Circle the word** *talk . . . talk.*

Scoring: For each child, mark the answer to each question correct or incorrect. Then count the total number correct for each child. Using the guidelines below, record the child's score in the Individual Record for the End-of-Year Assessment with alignments to Common Core State Standards (T96).

Number Correct	Rating	
11 – 12	Proficient	+
8 – 10	Developing	✓
Fewer than 8	Emerging	–

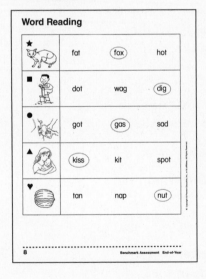

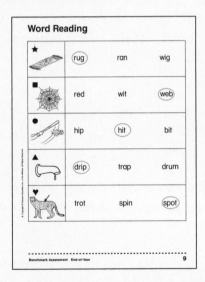

4. Word Knowledge: High-Frequency Words
(Individual or small group)

Purpose: Assesses ability to immediately recognize high-frequency words.

Hand out student pages 11–13. Children are to circle each word as you say it aloud. Move through the assessment quickly to make sure you are assessing the child's ability to recognize the high-frequency word quickly.

1. **I am going to say one word in each row. You are going to circle the word I say. Find the first row with the square in it. Put your finger on it. Now look at the three words in that row. Draw a circle around the word *with . . . with*.**

2. **Move down to the next row. Put your finger on the circle. Look at the three words. Circle the word *four . . . four*.**

3. **Move down to the next row. Put your finger on the triangle. Look at the three words. Circle the word *where . . . where*.**

4. **Move down to the next row. Put your finger on the heart. Look at the three words. Circle the word *me . . . me*.**

5. **Move down to the next row. Put your finger on the diamond. Look at the three words. Circle the word *green . . . green*.**

6. **Now go to the top of the next page. Look at the top row with the square in it. Put your finger on the square. Look at the three words. Circle the word *to . . . to*.**

7. **Move down to the next row. Put your finger on the circle. Look at the three words. Circle the word *one . . . one*.**

8. **Move down to the next row. Put your finger on the triangle. Look at the three words. Circle the word *said . . . said*.**

9. **Move down to the next row. Put your finger on the heart. Look at the three words. Circle the word *little . . . little*.**

10. Move down to the next row. Put your finger on the diamond. Look at the three words. Circle the word *that . . . that*.

11. Now go to the top of the next page. Look at the top row with the star in it. Put your finger on the star. Look at the three words. Circle the word *like . . . like*.

12. Move down to the next row. Put your finger on the square. Look at the three words. Circle the word *she . . . she*.

13. Move down to the next row. Put your finger on the oval. Look at the three words. Circle the word *have . . . have*.

14. Move down to the next row. Put your finger on the rectangle. Look at the three words. Circle the word *what . . . what*.

15. Move down to the next row. Put your finger on the diamond. Look at the three words. Circle the word *from . . . from*.

Scoring: For each child, count the total number of words circled correctly. Using the guidelines below, record the child's score on the Individual Record for the End-of-Year Benchmark Assessment with alignments to Common Core State Standards (T96).

Number Correct	Rating	
14 – 15	Proficient	+
11 – 13	Developing	✓
Fewer than 11	Emerging	–

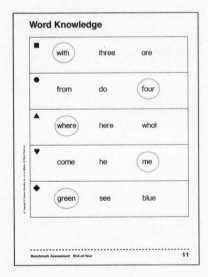

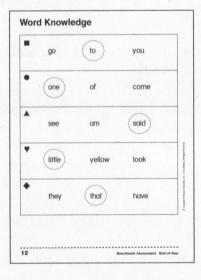

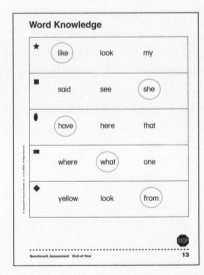

5. Listening Comprehension: Plot, Main Idea, Character, Setting

(Individual, small group, or whole class)

Purpose: Assesses general comprehension.

Hand out student page 14. Read aloud the introduction and the story printed in **bold.** Then read each question that follows. Children are to respond by circling the best answer to each question.

I am going to read a story about a pony named Clara. Then I will ask you some questions. Listen carefully. Here is the story.

Once upon a time there was a pretty pony named Clara. Clara belonged to the queen of a large kingdom. Clara lived in a big field filled with flowers. The queen came to visit Clara every day. She always gave Clara plenty of food. Clara loved being in her field, and she loved the queen. But she always felt a little sad. Clara felt lonely when the queen went home.

The queen knew Clara was sad. She wanted to make Clara happy. The queen brought Clara to a barn that was close to the castle. That way Clara could see the queen more. All day long Clara looked out of the window in the barn. She watched the queen all day. But Clara was still sad. She liked seeing the queen. But she didn't like being inside the barn all the time.

The queen saw that Clara was still not happy. She tried something new to make Clara happy. The queen brought Clara back to the field. Clara thought it was good to be outside again. She ran in the field and played in the flowers. Later that day the queen came back. She had a surprise for Clara. It was another pony! The new pony was named Belle. Clara and Belle became friends. They played together every day. Clara was never sad or lonely again.

Now I am going to ask you some questions about the story. For each question there are three pictures. Draw a circle around the picture that shows the best answer. Listen carefully.

1. **Look at the first row of pictures at the top of the page where you see the square. Put your finger on the square. How did Clara feel at the beginning of the story—happy, sad, or angry? Circle the picture that shows how Clara felt at the beginning of the story.**

2. **Move down to the next row of pictures where you see the circle. Put your finger on the circle. Where did Clara live at the beginning of the story? Circle the picture that shows where Clara lived at the beginning of the story.**

3. **Move down to the next row of pictures where you see the triangle. Put your finger on the triangle. What did the queen try to do first to make Clara feel happy? Circle the picture that shows what the queen first tried to do to make Clara happy.**

4. **Move down to the next row of pictures where you see the heart. Put your finger on the heart. What did Clara do all day long when she was in the barn? Circle the picture that shows what Clara did all day long when she was in the barn.**

5. **Move down to the last row of pictures where you see the rectangle. Put your finger on the rectangle. What made Clara happy? Circle the picture that shows what made Clara feel happy.**

Hand out student page 15. Read aloud the introduction and the story printed in **bold**. Then read each question that follows. Children are to respond by circling the best answer to each question.

Now I am going to read a story about a girl named Sara. Then I will ask you some questions. Listen carefully. Here is the story.

Sara woke up feeling happy. Today her family was going to the zoo. Sara was excited to see the animals. She thought the monkeys, the lions, and the zebras were fun to watch. But Ellie, the big gray elephant, was her favorite.

Sara had a special reason to visit Ellie today. Sara had a new toy elephant. It was a baby, and Sara wanted to show her toy elephant to the real elephant.

After breakfast, Sara and her parents got in the car and drove to the zoo.

When they arrived at the zoo, Sara led her parents to the elephant area. It was a big open space behind a tall fence. Sara looked and looked, but she didn't see Ellie. She felt so sad that she began to cry. Then her mother pointed to a sign. The sign said that Ellie was inside the elephant house. This seemed strange to Sara. It was warm and sunny outside. She wondered why Ellie was inside.

Sara and her parents walked into the elephant house and found a wonderful surprise. Ellie was not alone. Ellie was a mother now. She was standing next to her baby elephant. Ellie's baby looked just like Sara's toy. Sara held up her toy elephant for Ellie to see. Sara thought it was the best visit to the zoo!

Now I am going to ask you some questions about the story. For each question there are three pictures. Draw a circle around the picture that shows the best answer. Listen carefully.

6. Look at the first row of pictures at the top of the page where you see the square. Put your finger on the square. What happened first in the story? Circle the picture that shows what happened first in the story.

7. Move down to the next row of pictures where you see the circle. Put your finger on the circle. How did Sara's family get to the zoo? Circle the picture that shows how Sara's family got to the zoo.

8. Move down to the next row of pictures where you see the triangle. Put your finger on the triangle. What was Sara's favorite animal at the zoo? Circle the picture that shows Sara's favorite animal at the zoo.

9. Move down to the next row of pictures where you see the heart. Put your finger on the heart. How did Sara feel when she saw the empty elephant area—angry, happy, or sad? Circle the picture that shows how Sara felt when she saw the empty elephant area.

10. Move down to the last row of pictures where you see the rectangle. Put your finger on the rectangle. What did Sara see in the elephant house? Circle the picture that shows what Sara saw in the elephant house.

Scoring: For each child, mark the answer to each question correct or incorrect. Then count the total number correct for each child. Using the guidelines below, record the child's score in the Individual Record for the End-of-Year Assessment with alignments to Common Core State Standards (T96).

Number Correct	Rating	
9 – 10	Proficient	+
6 – 8	Developing	✓
Fewer than 6	Emerging	–

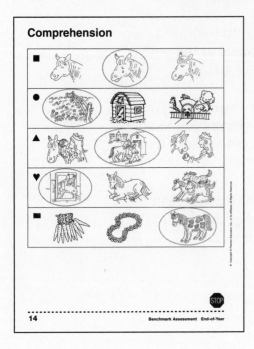

6. Writing: Nouns and Pronouns

(Individual, small group, or whole class)

Purpose: Assesses ability to write sentences.

Hand out student page 16. Instruct children as follows.

Now we are going to do something different. Remember that a noun is the name of a person, animal, place, or thing. Also remember that a pronoun is a word that is used in place of a noun. Draw a picture of something you like to eat. Then write a sentence or two about the picture. Use nouns and pronouns in your sentences.

Scoring: Use the guidelines below, evaluate the child's work, and record the child's score on the Individual Record for the End-of-Year Benchmark Assessment with alignments to Common Core State Standards (T96).

Scoring Guidelines	Rating	
The child draws a recognizable picture. The sentence or two contains a noun and pronouns, tells about the picture, and is generally written correctly.	Proficient	+
The child draws a reasonable picture. The sentence or two includes a noun and pronouns, but the words may include a few errors.	Developing	✓
The child draws a picture and attempts to write or dictate a sentence, but both are less than complete and correct.	Emerging	–

Writing

16   Benchmark Assessment   End-of-Year

INDIVIDUAL RECORD

End-of-Year Benchmark Assessment

Child's Name _____ **Date** _____

Directions: Record the results of the End-of-Year Benchmark Assessment by marking Proficient (+), Developing (✓), or Emerging (–) beside each assessed skill.

End-of-Year Assessed Skills	Proficient (+)	Developing (✓)	Emerging (–)	Common Core State Standard
Phonemic Awareness: Recognizing Initial and Final Sounds; Blending Individual Phonemes				Foundational Skills 2.c., 2.d.
Phonics: Letter-Sound Correspondence				Foundational Skills 3.a., 3.b.
Word Reading: CVC, CVCC, CCVC Words				Foundational Skills 3.
Word Knowledge: High-Frequency Words				Foundational Skills 3.c.
Listening Comprehension: Plot, Main Idea, Character, Setting				Literature 3.
Writing: Nouns and Pronouns				Writing 2.

CLASS RECORD CHART

Skills Assessment   Unit _____

Teacher's Name _____ Date _____

Directions: Use this chart to record the results for all children on any of the Unit Benchmark Assessments or the End-of-Year Assessment. Fill in the number of the unit at the top. Beside each child's name, record the results by marking Proficient (+), Developing (✓), or Emerging (−) under each assessed skill.

Child's Name	Phonemic Awareness	Phonological Awareness	Letter Naming	Phonics	Word Knowledge	Word Reading	Comprehension	Writing
1.								
2.								
3.								
4.								
5.								
6.								
7.								
8.								
9.								
10.								
11.								
12.								
13.								
14								
15								
16.								
17.								
18.								
19.								
20.								
21.								
22.								
23.								
24.								

NAME _____ DATE _____

Scott Foresman
Benchmark Assessment
Unit 1
All Together Now

PEARSON

Glenview, Illinois
Boston, Massachusetts
Chandler, Arizona
Upper Saddle River, New Jersey

ISBN-13: 978-0-328-53707-5
ISBN-10:   0-328-53707-1
1 2 3 4 5 6 7 8 9 10 V016 19 18 17 16 15 14 13 12 11 10
CC1

ISBN-13: 978-0-328-53707-5
ISBN-10:   0-328-53707-1
EAN
9 780328 537075
90000 >

Letter Naming

M	r	T	u	p	R	P	f	A
S	G	b	E	K	o	w	n	Z
y	a	W	N	L	e	d	h	s
V	q	O	i	z	U	g	m	v
D	c	X	J	F	Q	j	x	C
H	k	B	l	Y	I	t		

STOP

Benchmark Assessment Unit 1

Phonological Awareness

Word Knowledge

am

the

I

little

to

a

STOP

Comprehension

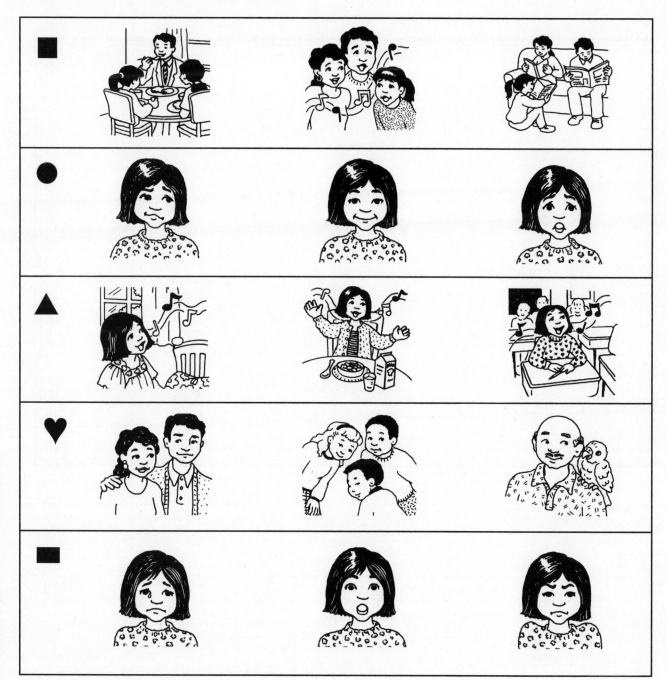

STOP

Writing

STOP

NAME _____   DATE _____

Scott Foresman
Benchmark Assessment
Unit 2
Look at Us!

Glenview, Illinois
Boston, Massachusetts
Chandler, Arizona
Upper Saddle River, New Jersey

ISBN-13: 978-0-328-53708-2
ISBN-10:   0-328-53708-x
1 2 3 4 5 6 7 8 9 10 V016 19 18 17 16 15 14 13 12 11 10
CC1

ISBN-13: 978-0-328-53708-2
ISBN-10:   0-328-53708-X

EAN

9 780328 537082

90000>

Phonemic Awareness

Phonemic Awareness

STOP

Phonics

★ (safety pin)	a u i
■ (map)	m b r
● (top)	s t f
▲ (rug)	e a o
♥ (sock)	s n d

Phonics

■	t k p
●	f s c
▲	i e u

STOP

Word Knowledge

★	have	am	the
■	a	like	is
●	we	I	am
▲	he	my	we
♥	the	little	like
▪	he	me	we
◆	little	for	to

Comprehension

STOP

Writing

NAME _____ DATE _____

Scott Foresman
Benchmark Assessment
Unit 3
Changes All Around Us

Glenview, Illinois
Boston, Massachusetts
Chandler, Arizona
Upper Saddle River, New Jersey

ISBN-13: 978-0-328-53709-9
ISBN-10:   0-328-53709-8
1 2 3 4 5 6 7 8 9 10 V016 19 18 17 16 15 14 13 12 11 10
CC1

ISBN-13: 978-0-328-53709-9
ISBN-10:   0-328-53709-8

Phonemic Awareness

Phonemic Awareness

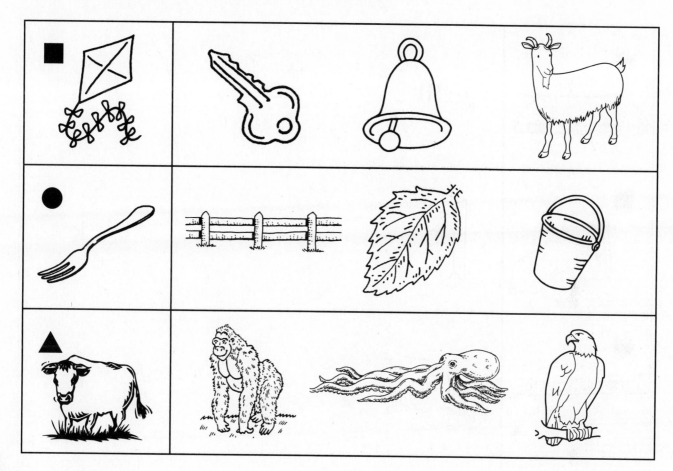

STOP

Phonics

★ 	m	c	r
■ 	b	t	k
● 	s	d	n
▲ 	c	s	r
♥ 	f	d	p

Phonics

■	t k g
●	f h j
▲	u i o

STOP

Word Knowledge

★	am	me	the
■	with	mat	we
●	she	sit	he
▲	little	look	ball
♥	cat	sun	see
■	have	met	they
◆	you	my	yes
⬮	a	of	for

STOP

Comprehension

STOP

Writing

NAME _____   DATE _____

Scott Foresman
Benchmark Assessment
Unit 4
Let's Go Exploring

Glenview, Illinois
Boston, Massachusetts
Chandler, Arizona
Upper Saddle River, New Jersey

ISBN-13: 978-0-328-53710-5
ISBN-10:   0-328-53710-1
1 2 3 4 5 6 7 8 9 10 V016 19 18 17 16 15 14 13 12 11 10
CC1

ISBN-13: 978-0-328-53710-5
ISBN-10:   0-328-53710-1

EAN

9 780328 537105

90000>

Phonemic Awareness

Phonemic Awareness

STOP

Phonics

★	dr	bl	tr
■	st	sp	dr
●	bl	dr	br
▲	h	l	g
♥	a	e	o

Phonics

■	r	s	h
●	f	l	g
▲	sp	st	lk
♥	st	lk	sp

STOP

Word Reading

★ [cat image]	cat cot cap
■ [bed image]	bat bet bed
● [hat image]	hat ham hit
▲ [net image]	tan net not
♥ [top image]	top dot pet
■ [pin image]	pot pig pin

STOP

Word Knowledge

★	am	are	red
■	mat	the	that
●	do	you	to
▲	one	not	go
♥	they	you	two
▬	we	three	the
◆	fan	of	four
⬮	five	like	have

Word Knowledge

■	we	here	he
●	get	he	go
▲	for	from	my

STOP

Comprehension

STOP

Writing

Scott Foresman
Benchmark Assessment

Unit 5
Going Places

PEARSON

Glenview, Illinois
Boston, Massachusetts
Chandler, Arizona
Upper Saddle River, New Jersey

ISBN-13: 978-0-328-53711-2
ISBN-10:   0-328-53711-X

1 2 3 4 5 6 7 8 9 10 V016 19 18 17 16 15 14 13 12 11 10
CC1

ISBN-13: 978-0-328-53711-2
ISBN-10:   0-328-53711-X

Phonemic Awareness

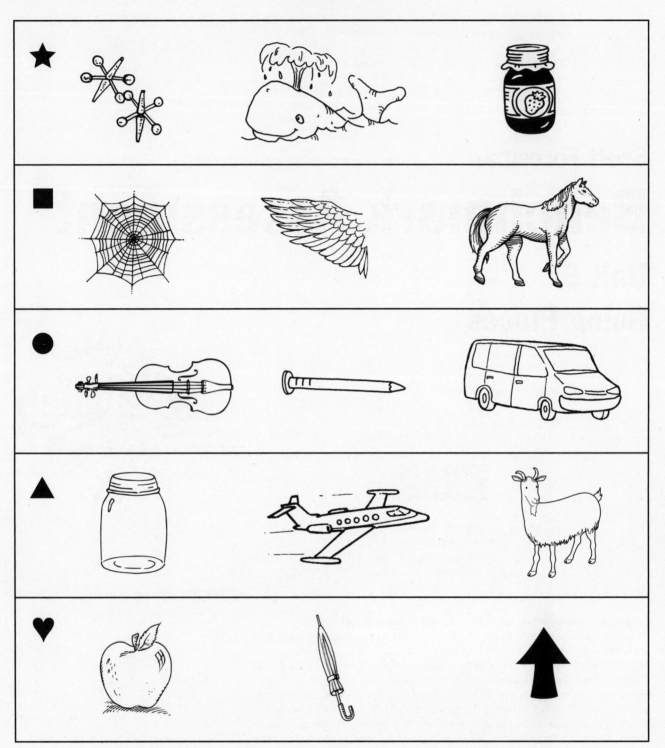

Phonemic Awareness

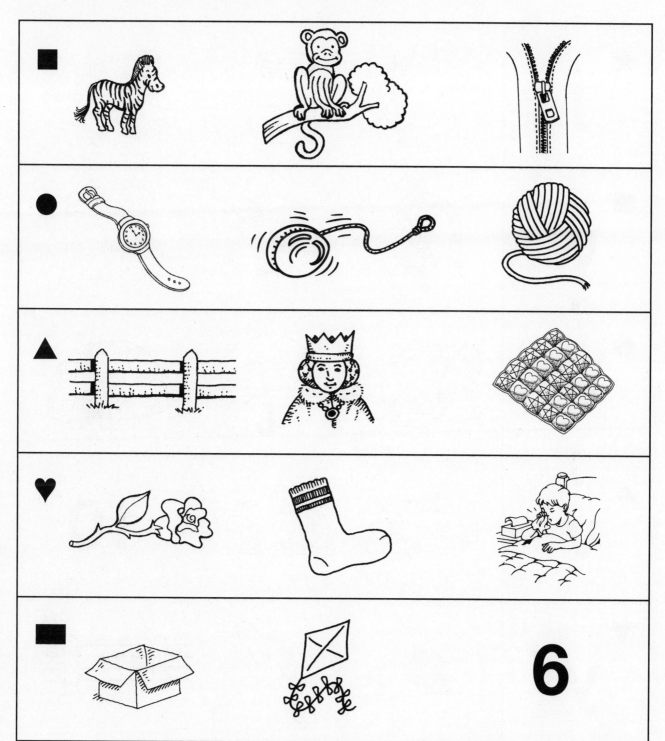

Phonics

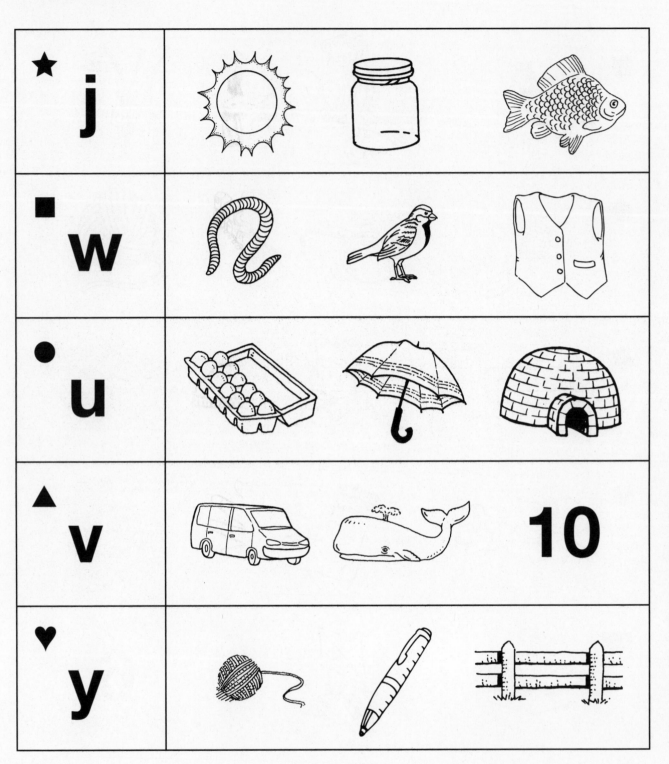

Phonics

■ **qu**			
● **j**			
▲ **x**			
♥ **z**			

STOP

Word Reading

★	can	pet	cup
■	pin	nap	big
●	bat	pat	bag
▲ **10**	net	ten	top
♥	dot	bed	box

Word Reading

■	*(log)*	dog	log	led
●	*(man)*	man	mud	mop
▲	*(sun)*	sat	sun	ran
♥	*(bib)*	bad	bud	bib

STOP

Word Knowledge

■	yellow	yes	you
●	go	ten	green
▲	blue	look	you
♥	with	we	what
▬	have	said	see
◆	was	what	one
⬤	here	they	where
⬢	can	come	my

Comprehension

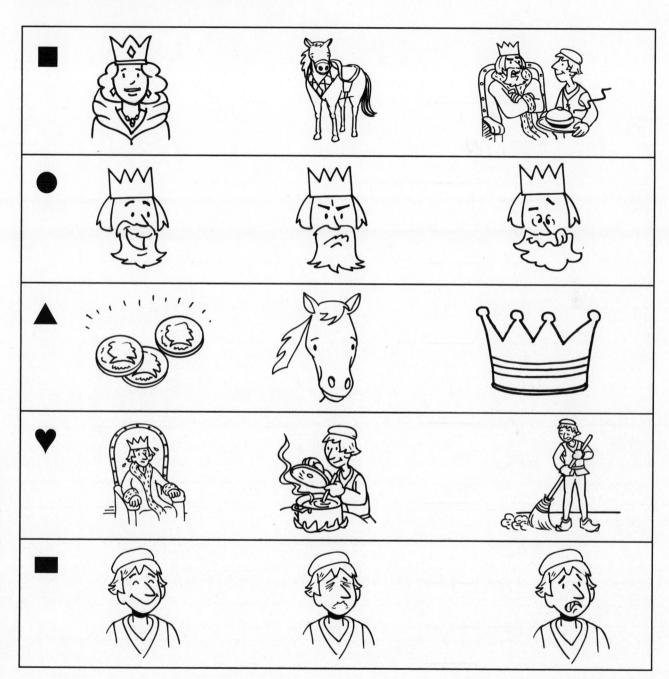

STOP

Writing

NAME _____ DATE _____

Scott Foresman
Benchmark Assessment
Unit 6
Putting It Together

PEARSON

Glenview, Illinois
Boston, Massachusetts
Chandler, Arizona
Upper Saddle River, New Jersey

ISBN-13: 978-0-328-53712-9
ISBN-10:   0-328-53712-8

1 2 3 4 5 6 7 8 9 10 V016 19 18 17 16 15 14 13 12 11 10
CC1

ISBN-13: 978-0-328-53712-9
ISBN-10:   0-328-53712-8

EAN

9 780328 537129

Phonemic Awareness

Phonemic Awareness

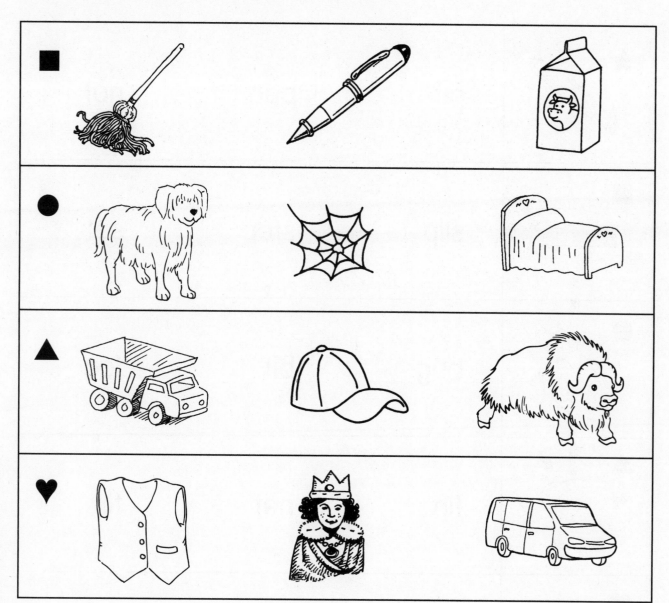

STOP

Word Reading

★	pit	pen	not
■	slip	step	set
●	bug	bit	tag
▲	fin	net	fill
♥	bat	bump	box

Word Reading

■	quit	jet	jug
●	map	pan	mat
▲	trap	tub	tin
♥	fast	drag	van

STOP

Word Knowledge

■	green	go	of
●	said	she	is
▲	look	come	from
♥	are	for	am
▬	the	what	two
◆	with	five	have
⬤	go	do	you

Word Knowledge

■	here	little	green
●	we	what	where
▲	one	of	am

STOP

Comprehension

Benchmark Assessment Unit 6

STOP

Writing

NAME _____ DATE _____

Scott Foresman
Benchmark Assessment
End-of-Year

Reading STREET
Grade K

Glenview, Illinois
Boston, Massachusetts
Chandler, Arizona
Upper Saddle River, New Jersey

ISBN-13: 978-0-328-53713-6
ISBN-10:   0-328-53713-6

1 2 3 4 5 6 7 8 9 10 V016 19 18 17 16 15 14 13 12 11 10
CC1

ISBN-13: 978-0-328-53713-6
ISBN-10:   0-328-53713-6

Phonemic Awareness

Phonemic Awareness

Phonemic Awareness

Benchmark Assessment   End-of-Year

Phonics

★ **r**	ring	umbrella	van
■ **d**	dog	queen	tape
● **v**	book	train	vine
▲ **f**	bird	fan	car
♥ **n**	9	bee	clock

Phonics

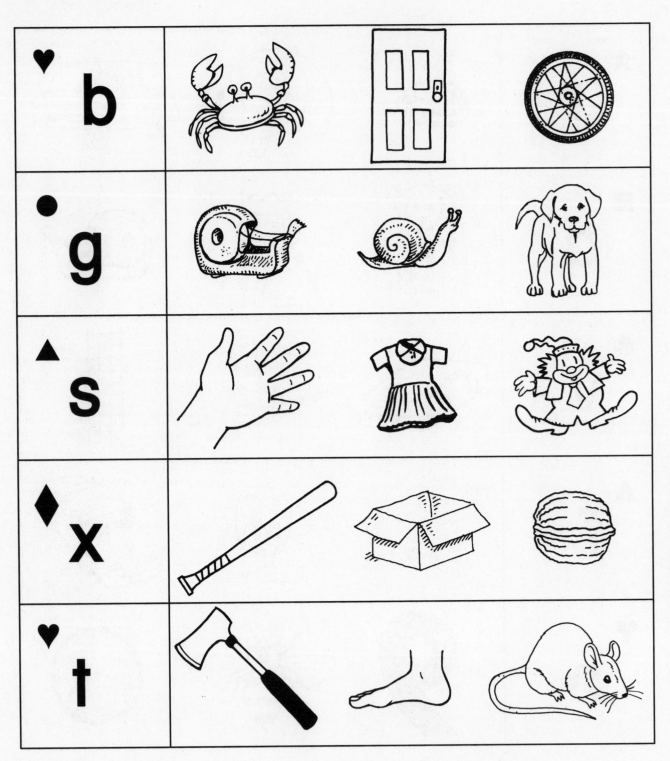

Benchmark Assessment   End-of-Year

Phonics

★ (block)	**bl** **sp** **st**
■ (egg)	**u** **a** **e**
● (yarn)	**n** **y** **l**
▲ (drum)	**st** **dr** **br**
♥ (bee)	**sp** **k** **st**

Word Reading

★	fat	fox	hot
■	dot	wag	dig
●	got	gas	sad
▲	kiss	kit	spot
♥	tan	nap	nut

Word Reading

★ *(rug image)*	rug	ran	wig
■ *(web image)*	red	wit	web
● *(bat hitting ball image)*	hip	hit	bit
▲ *(drip image)*	drip	trap	drum
♥ *(cheetah image)*	trot	spin	spot

Word Reading

■	tin	trip	pat
●	vest	jet	last
▲	fall	top	talk

STOP

Word Knowledge

■	with	three	are
●	from	do	four
▲	where	here	what
♥	come	he	me
◆	green	see	blue

Word Knowledge

■	go	to	you
●	one	of	come
▲	see	am	said
♥	little	yellow	look
◆	they	that	have

Word Knowledge

★	like	look	my
■	said	see	she
●	have	here	that
▬	where	what	one
◆	yellow	look	from

STOP

Comprehension

STOP

Benchmark Assessment   End-of-Year

Comprehension

STOP

Writing

STOP